Complete
Handyman
do-it-yourself
Encyclopedia

do-it-

low yield

medium yield

high yield

minimum effort

needs more care

requires special attention

crops in three months or less

crops in 4-12 months

crops in over 12 months

Complete Handyman
yourself
Encyclopedia

A STEP BY STEP GUIDE TO SUCCESSFUL
VEGETABLE AND FRUIT GROWING
BASED ON ALL 52 GARDENING HANDBOOKS
PUBLISHED UNDER THE TITLE

GROW YOUR OWN

VOLUME
22
APPLES
BRUSSELS SPROUTS

H. S. STUTTMAN INC.   *Publishers*   **WESTPORT, CONN.**

Based on the gardening handbooks
"GROW YOUR OWN"
Copyright © 1977
Marshall Cavendish Ltd.

PRINTED IN THE UNITED STATES OF AMERICA
3P(199)30-90

Introduction

WITH THE COMPLETION of Volumes 22 to 26, the COMPLETE HANDYMAN ENCYCLOPEDIA becomes an even more essential addition to the home. These GROW YOUR OWN volumes provide step-by-step guidance to the successful growing of practically every known fruit, vegetable or herb.

Most good gardening books in print *tell* you how; but GROW YOUR OWN—with its full-color step-by-step illustrations—*shows* you how to do every gardening chore. Whether you want to know how to sprout seed potatoes for planting . . . how to plant peas . . . or all about pinching back tomato suckers to assure big, juicy, plump tomatoes . . . you'll find detailed, full-color sequential pictures that walk you through each job just as if you had an expert "looking over your shoulder."

Step-by-step growing guides provide detailed and comprehensive instructions to grow each important garden crop to perfection. Everything from sowing to harvesting is shown in step-by-step illustrations. Important techniques are explained, as well as a guide to varieties of each crop. Advice on preventing the ravages of pests and diseases pertinent to each crop is another key to gardening success.

Growing ideas bring you a variety of interesting new projects . . . high-yield vegetables you may have overlooked . . . an exciting fruit to try . . . tips on how to grow your own fresh herbs. The more experienced gardeners will discover a wealth of ideas that increase their range, while beginners will appreciate the information on growing quick and easy crops.

In planning Volumes 22 to 26 of the COMPLETE HANDYMAN ENCYCLOPEDIA, the publishers were fortunate in having the editorial assistance and guidance of Edwin F. Steffek, Editor Emeritus of the magazine Horticulture. We wish to express our gratitude to him for his diligence in editing and writing new material with the objective of making this edition of GROW YOUR OWN a most valuable and useful part of your COMPLETE HANDYMAN ENCYCLOPEDIA.

Whether you are already a gardening expert, or are testing the greenness of your thumb for the very first time, now you have a garden helper to bring you a more productive, more rewarding, garden! GROW YOUR OWN is different because it's designed to give you *fast* answers and advice about every gardening question.

H. S. STUTTMAN INC.
Publishers

Contents

VOLUME ... 24

VOLUME ... 25

VOLUME . . . 26

Apples

Malus pumila (fam. *Rosaceae*)
Hardy deciduous tree, with a useful life of about 50 years
Planting to harvesting time: dwarf trees on M9 rootstock produce fruit when about three years old. More vigorous trees take a year or so longer
Size: from about 6 ft (1.8 m) tall for dwarf trees to about 25 ft (7.5 m) for standard trees. Up to 40 ft (12 m) for crab apples
Yield: dwarf trees may average about 30 lb (14 kg) a year; semidwarf trees, 60 lb (28 kg), and mature larger trees may even reach half a ton (500 kg)

The apple is probably the most widely grown tree fruit because it is decidedly hardy and there are varieties to suit most soil and weather conditions. Even a neglected apple tree will produce some kind of crop, but all too often the wormy or diseased fruit harvested from neglected trees could easily be avoided. With a little care, a mature tree can be restored to vigorous cropping within a couple of seasons and will supply the family with large supplies of delicious fruit.

Apples are a rewarding crop to grow in the small garden. It does not take long for a young tree to start fruiting; dwarfing rootstock can be chosen to restrict the size of the tree so that it will not outgrow its site; a small number of trees will provide all the apples that a family will want, and careful selection of varieties can ensure fruit almost all year round.

The trees will grow happily in most temperate regions. They need a sunny, well-drained site which is sheltered and frost-free at blossom time to ensure that insects can pollinate. They will not grow in gardens waterlogged for long periods, although there is a way of overcoming this problem, as explained later. Some apples are more tolerant than others of heavy clay soil, high rainfall and indifferent drainage—and they can survive with less sunshine.

Types of apple
Apples can be divided into three groups: cooking apples, dessert (or eating) apples and crab apples. The last group can be planted as a pollinator for the others.

Cookers are sharply flavored and are not usually eaten raw. They tend to have a longer season, to keep better and are more tolerant of less-than-perfect conditions than most other varieties. However, most growers prefer dual-purpose varieties, both cooking and eating.

Sweeter in flavor, and mainly eaten raw, are the dessert apples. These are smaller than cooking apples and have a shorter eating season. The trees dislike rainfall of more than 40 in (1 m) a year.

Harry Smith

⋏ A modern dwarf apple tree—convenient to look after and ideal for the small garden.

Choosing trees

Combination cooking and dessert apples suit most families best. Some apple trees must have another variety nearby flowering at the same time, if they are to bear fruit, so you should plant a minimum of two. Most varieties have plenty of pollen and will pollinate one another, provided their flowering seasons coincide or overlap. Some have little pollen—they are known as triploid and need a suitable pollinator to set their fruit. Triploids will not pollinate the other tree, however, so in this case there may be a third variety present (not triploid) to ensure a good crop on all three.

A very few varieties are self-fertile but all will give bigger crops if pollinated by another.

Tree shapes: the simplest and most appropriate form of tree for the small garden is the dwarf. These small, free-standing trees are simple to manage and the fruit can be easily harvested. For very small sites they can sometimes even be planted in as little as 5 ft (1.5 m) of space.

Apples trees can, however, be trained in several different shapes, some of which are particularly useful. Cordons are excellent space savers grown on walls or fences, or can be used in a row as a screen. Fans are also suitable for a large wall, but apple trees should not be placed in too warm a site. The espalier, with branches trained at regular intervals at right angles from the trunk, and dwarf pyramid trees are also possible.

If you want to train a tree into one of these artificial shapes, you must buy a maiden—a one-year-old. The inexperienced gardener may find it easier to buy a ready trained tree, two or three years old, from the nurseryman. Maintaining the shape is then relatively simple. Training cordon trees is explained later.

Rootstocks: nowadays trees are formed by joining the apple variety to a separate root system or "stock." The fruiting

TREE SHAPES

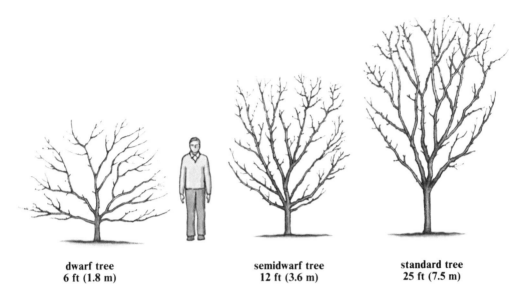

**dwarf tree
6 ft (1.8 m)**   **semidwarf tree
12 ft (3.6 m)**   **standard tree
25 ft (7.5 m)**

habit of the resulting tree is that of the top, called the scion, but the size is determined by the rootstock.

The development of what are called dwarfing rootstocks means that now small trees are available which fruit abundantly. The research was carried out at East Malling Research Station and at Merton in England and their rootstocks, referred to as M (Malling) and MM (Malling Merton), are used throughout the world. By choosing between rootstocks you can select the variety you want at the size you want. For instance, M9 rootstock produces the most dwarf trees; MM106 and M7 semidwarf specimens. If you are buying a tree, the nursery catalog will explain the differences in detail.

There are trees available with several varieties (usually three) grafted on to the same roots. These "family trees" are particularly suitable where space is very limited. The three varieties will pollinate each other and you will have a selection of types of apple.

Age of tree: if you intend to train an apple on a fence or wall yourself, buy a maiden (one-year-old tree). You will, however, get fruit sooner by buying a two- or three-year-old cordon type. But do not let trees bear more than one or two sample fruit each in their first summer—give the roots time to reestablish.

Preparing the soil
A medium loam, slightly acid and well-drained, is the perfect type of soil.

If possible, prepare the soil in summer by deep digging to improve surface drainage and get rid of perennial weeds. If you cannot prepare the soil so far in advance, firm the ground well by treading or rolling it after digging. Then leave it to settle for two weeks or more before planting.

If the soil is very acid make it less so by applying lime. Improve a neutral or only just alkaline soil by working in manure and use acid fertilizers such as sulfate of ammonia when necessary. The lack of nutrients caused by highly alkaline soil can be corrected by modern artificial fertilizers and foliar sprays.

Work in liberal quantities of manure, compost, peat or leafmold to improve the consistency of light, sandy or gravelly soil, and do the same thing for heavy clay soils.

If you are planning to grow apples in a kitchen garden where there has been a high level of feeding, beware! Tree growth, especially of some varieties, will be stimulated to the detriment of fruit blossom. Delay tree-planting for a year, meanwhile do not fertilize the ground but go on growing vegetables.

Planting
Planting is possible at any time during the dormant season—when there are no leaves on the tree—so long as the ground is neither frozen hard nor too wet to work freely. The soil should be crumbly, not pasty. Late fall and spring are best.

Plant the trees as soon as they are delivered, if possible. If the roots have dried out in transit soak them in water in a large can for about an hour. Trim back any damaged roots, making slanting cuts on the underside of thicker roots.

If for any reason planting has to be delayed, heel trees in temporarily in the open. Make a trench, with one side sloping at an angle of about 45°, deep enough to bury the roots up to the soil mark on the stem, which shows the depth to which the tree was growing in the nursery. Lay the tree in this trench and cover the roots with soil just up to the soil mark. Tread in lightly.

The trees should not be planted too close together. For those trees on semi-dwarf rootstock in average quality soil, allow a radius of 7 ft (2.2 m) around each. In rich soil, increase this to 9 ft (2.8 m). Standard trees more likely need 20 ft (6 m) or more for best growth. For the smallest trees on M9 rootstock, allow a radius of 5 ft (1.5 m) and for vigorous growers on dwarf M9 rootstock, 6 ft (1.8 m). Multivariety trees usually need more space, up to 14 ft (4.2 m).

Try to get someone to help you when you plant the trees. An extra pair of hands will make it much easier to position a tree straight and upright. Dig each planting hole wide and deep enough for all the roots to be spread out fully in their natural growing position. When you have finished planting and treading down the soil, the tree should be at exactly the same soil depth as it was when growing in the nursery. The join of the rootstock and the scion (called the

union) must not be below ground level, or the scion may put out its own rootstock.

To check that your planting hole is of the right depth, lay a stick across it to show you the ground level and hold the tree in its planting position in the hole. The level of the stick should match the mark on the stem of the soil from its former planting.

All dwarf trees need staking. Use 2 in (5 cm) diameter stakes which have been treated with a copper-based preservative. Drive two upright stakes into the planting hole, each about 9 in (23 cm) away from the tree. In light soil they'll eventually be buried 2 ft (60 cm) below soil level, in heavy soil 1½ ft (45 cm).

Put a spadeful of soil into the bottom of the hole, spread out the roots, sprinkle over a few handfuls of moist peat and start returning the soil. If soil is rather poor, mix a couple of handfuls of sterilized bonemeal (superphosphate is now considered far superior) with the soil waiting to go back into the planting hole, but not in immediate contact with the roots. Get a helper to wriggle the tree a little so the soil filters well between the roots. Tread the soil down to firm it as you go.

Water with one 2½ gal (12 L) bucketful and, if there is no rain within a week, give it another bucketful.

Level off the soil and surround the tree as far as the branches extend with a surface mulch of well-rotted compost, manure, leafmold or damp peat, but do not let this touch the tree stem or it may rot the bark.

As soon as the tree is planted fix a crosspiece to the two stakes, a little below the lowest branch, and fasten the tree to it. Use a ready-made plastic tree-tie for this job, or wrap a piece of sacking or cloth around the tree to protect the bark and tie over it with soft string. Finish by twisting the string between the tree and stake to prevent chafing.

During the early months the soil will settle and the tie may need repositioning. In two or three years the tree may be able to dispense with support.

Step-by-step Growing Guide for Apples

PLANTING A TREE

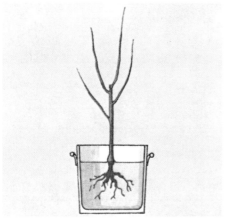

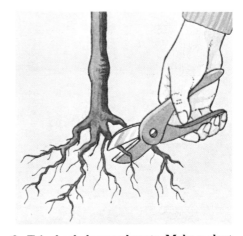

1. If roots have dried out, soak in water for about an hour.

2. Trim back damaged roots. Make a slanting cut in thicker roots.

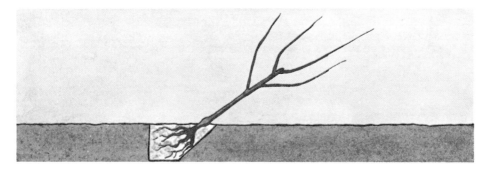

3. If planting is delayed, bury roots in a trench, up to soil mark on stem.

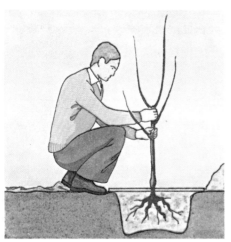

4. Place stick across hole to check planting depth. Soil mark on stem should align with the stick.

5. Drive in upright stakes 9 in (23 cm) away from tree. Return soil, making sure it penetrates between the roots.

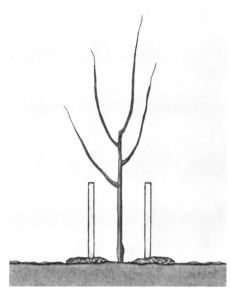

6. Tread the soil down firmly and level off. Make sure the union of rootstock and scion is above ground.

7. Apply surface mulch of rotted compost, manure or peat, but avoid touching the stem.

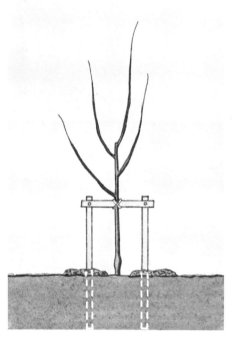

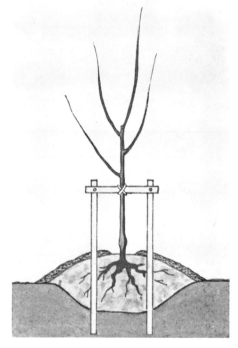

8. Erect a crosspiece between the stakes, to run below the bottom branch of the tree. Tie the tree to the crosspiece.

9. Planting method for badly drained ground: create a mound above a shallow hole to raise tree roots above the normal level.

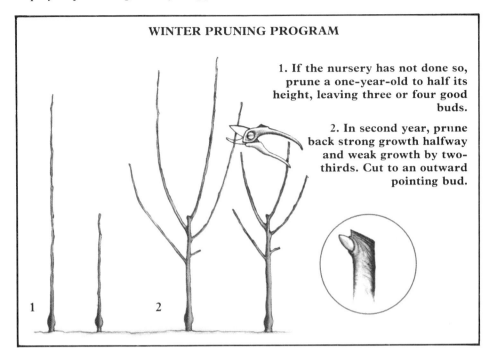

WINTER PRUNING PROGRAM

1. If the nursery has not done so, prune a one-year-old to half its height, leaving three or four good buds.

2. In second year, prune back strong growth halfway and weak growth by two-thirds. Cut to an outward pointing bud.

Planting on badly drained land
If you want to grow apples and the ground is badly drained, you can plant on a slight mound.

Make only a shallow depression instead of digging a deep planting hole. Stand the tree in this, insert its stakes and then mound up soil from some other part of the garden to the soil mark on the stem. The mound must be wider than the existing extent of the roots to encourage them to grow outwards. Mulching extends further than the branches and therefore each year you will have to top-dress further out.

This method can be used also where shallow topsoil overlies rock at a depth of about 1½ ft (45 cm).

Trees grown on mounds are more vulnerable to drought, and plenty of watering is essential in dry periods, particularly in early life. A mulch of compost or leafmold to arrest surface evaporation is very important.

Watering and feeding
The first year is a critical time for newly planted trees. In the first few summers it is essential to water freely and in adequate quantities, and a surface mulch will do much to conserve moisture in the soil.

Give no more manure in the first season. In succeeding winters, dress the ground around each tree a little further out than the branches extend. Use 1¼ oz per sq yd (38 g per sq m) of sulfate of ammonia and ¾ oz per sq yd (22 g per sq m) of sulfate of potash. Rake the fertilizers into the surface in late winter.

Thereafter, every other year rake in, at the same time, 1¾ oz per sq yd (52 g per sq m) of superphosphate. If the harvest has been heavy, an extra fertilizer dressing is beneficial.

Pruning
Winter pruning is to build a framework of robust main branches. Standards, semidwarfs and dwarfs are pruned the same way.

Immediately after planting give the tree its first pruning with sharp shears. Hard winter pruning stimulates the wood growth necessary at this stage of the tree's development. If it is an unpruned maiden tree cut it back to half its height, leaving three or four good buds.

If you have bought a two-year-old tree, it will have only three or four branches. If these are strong and long, cut each back half way, making your cut close beyond a growth bud pointing outward.

If these first branches are thin and wispy and not very long, be more drastic and cut off two-thirds of the length of each. This cutting back will cause growth buds near the cut ends to develop.

By the tree's third winter each of the primary branches will have made three or more secondary branches. Cut back the previous summer's growth by a third if strong, by a half if thin and wispy.

Some sideshoots (the laterals) may have grown from the secondary branches by now. If these laterals are badly placed to make new branches, cut each back to its fourth bud. Any sideshoots springing from the trunk of the tree just below the main branches should be sliced off flush with the stem.

Four-year-old dwarfs are regarded as adult. From now on winter pruning is restricted to the minimum necessary to ensure a continuing supply of fruiting wood, rather than to extend the size of the tree. Remove crossing branches and cankerous or broken ones.

If you do not prune a sideshoot, it will make fruit buds in its second year. These are bigger, fatter and rounder than growth buds and the next year will blossom in spring. Every winter leave at least some sideshoots unpruned to bear fruit. If more sideshoots are needed, cut back some to the second bud from the base. But, in general, cut back just the three-year-old sideshoots which have fruited to a 2 in (5 cm) stump.

Do not touch the tips of the branches once fruit-bearing has begun—unless a branch is growing in an undesirable direction and you want to replace the season's new extension growth (the leader) with another one. Some varieties also form fruit buds at the tips of one-year-old shoots. Leave such shoots intact.

THINNING FRUITLETS

Thin dessert apples to improve size and appearance of fruit. Use a thin pointed pair of scissors and cut out the central fruitlet in each cluster and then any diseased or smaller fruitlets. Leave only one or two fruit on each cluster.

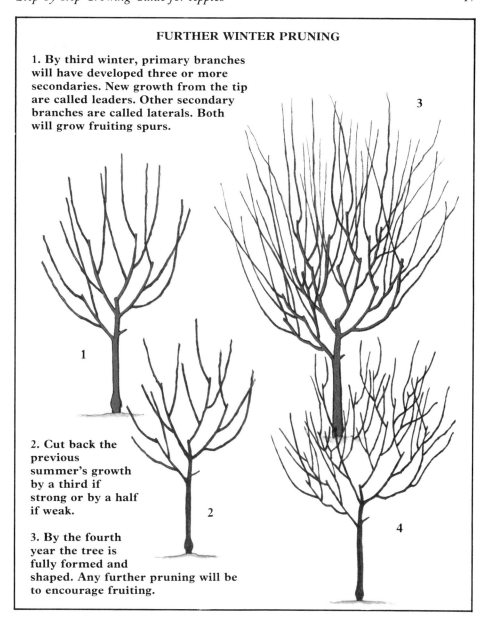

FURTHER WINTER PRUNING

1. By third winter, primary branches will have developed three or more secondaries. New growth from the tip are called leaders. Other secondary branches are called laterals. Both will grow fruiting spurs.

2. Cut back the previous summer's growth by a third if strong or by a half if weak.

3. By the fourth year the tree is fully formed and shaped. Any further pruning will be to encourage fruiting.

This system of pruning will produce a balance of fruiting laterals and vegetating ones to provide fruit later on.

Training cordons

A cordon consists of a single stem bearing fruiting spurs. The tree is planted at an angle to restrict growth and to encourage early fruiting and an even production of buds.

Rows should run from south to north if at all possible. Put in 7½ ft (2.3 m) sturdy posts, about 10 ft (3 m) apart. Stretch three heavy gauge galvanized wires between posts at heights of 2 ft (60 cm), 4 ft (1.2 m) and 6 ft (1.8 m). Use an adjustable turnbuckle at the end of each wire to keep it taut. Fix a long bamboo cane, 8 ft (2.4 m), to the wires at an angle of 45° where each tree is to be planted.

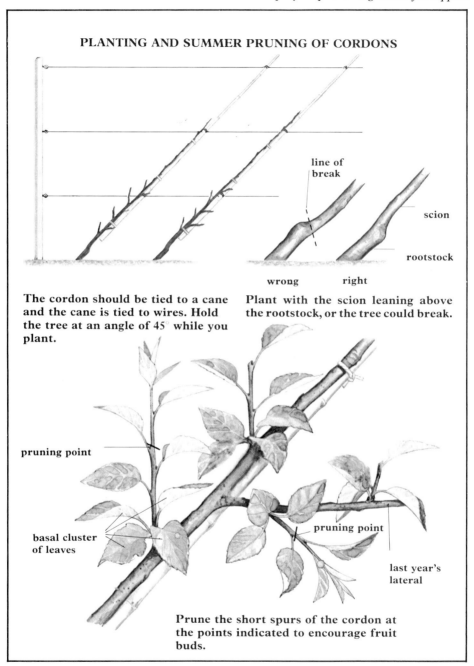

PLANTING AND SUMMER PRUNING OF CORDONS

line of break

scion

rootstock

wrong   right

The cordon should be tied to a cane and the cane is tied to wires. Hold the tree at an angle of 45° while you plant.

Plant with the scion leaning above the rootstock, or the tree could break.

pruning point

pruning point

basal cluster of leaves

last year's lateral

Prune the short spurs of the cordon at the points indicated to encourage fruit buds.

Plant two- to three-year-old cordons 2½ ft (75 cm) apart at an angle of 45° with the tip pointing away from the midday sun. Space rows 6 ft (1.8 m) apart.

About 4 in (10 cm) from the soil mark there is a swelling where the scion is joined to the rootstock. This is the union. Hold the whole tree at an angle for planting with the scion uppermost on the rootstock. Planted the other way around the tree could break off its roots.

As soon as it is planted, the cordon

must be tied to its supporting bamboo cane. Tie in three places—the lowest one 2 in (5 cm) above the union.

Pruning cordons
Pruning is necessary in the first winter for tip-bearing types. With these, cut back just the main stem by a quarter of the previous season's growth. Repeat in subsequent winters.

The main pruning is done in midsummer in warmer districts and up to a month later in cooler ones. Start when you see that sideshoots growing directly from the main cordon stem are maturing—when they are more than 9 in (23 cm) long, the leaves have lost their early brightness and become a deep green and the skin of the shoot has stiffened and begun to look barklike for the lower part of its length.

At the base of such shoots you will usually find a cluster of leaves. Ignore these, count three leaves from the base of the shoot and then cut close after the third leaf. There may also be growths springing from laterals made and pruned in a previous year. Cut each back to the first leaf beyond the basal cluster. If some new shoots are not mature, wait until they are before pruning. If secondary growth occurs in late summer from near the point where you made the first cuts, prune such shoots back to one leaf or bud in midautumn.

In about three years, when the cordon reaches the length of its cane, unfasten the cane from the wires and bend the whole tree down about 5° and refasten the cane. Repeat again in a few years if it appears to be necessary.

Usually there comes a time when the mature tree stops producing further extension growth each summer. But if it reaches the limit of space before this happens, cut it back in spring soon after new growth begins.

Except in the case of tip-bearing varieties, the leader should not normally be pruned until it must be checked for lack of space. If the desired fruit-bearing sideshoots are scarce, however, stimulate the production of more by pruning the

season's new extension growth of the leader by one third in winter. To encourage individual buds in a bare length of stem, cut a half-moon notch from the bark just above them.

If after some years there are too many fruiting spurs and they are getting crowded, in winter cut some back and take out others entirely.

Thinning out the fruit
If an apple tree bears a very heavy crop in any one year, it may take a rest the next season. The big crop, too, is likely to be of undersized fruit.

Many apples are thinned out to improve the appearance and size of the individual fruit. Others tend to be naturally larger and are not usually thinned. Fruit thinning is less likely to be required on dwarf trees growing on M9 rootstock and trees trained as cordons.

Some shedding of fruit occurs naturally about midsummer or just after, but the earlier you do any thinning the better for the tree. As soon as the fruitlets have "set" (when a tiny but obvious fruitlet has replaced the blossom and you know a heavy crop is possible) take a thin pointed pair of scissors and cut out the central fruitlet from each cluster. This "king apple" is sometimes misshapen and competes with the other fruit. Remove any blemished fruitlets and continue thinning until only one or two fruit remain out of each cluster. These fruit should never be closer than 4 in (10 cm) to the next cluster.

Supporting the branches
When the crop is heavy, branches may be broken by the weight of fruit. Watch out for this and support any which are likely to be affected. Either prop up the branches with forked stakes or drive in a stake close to the tree's stem and tie heavily laden branches to the top of it.

Harvesting the crop
When you think an apple is ripe, lift it in the palm of your hand and give it the slightest possible twist. If it comes away easily, it is ready. Dessert and cooking

Valerie Finnis

⋏ *A row of cordons is an excellent method of growing apples in a limited space.*

apples must be handled with care as they are easily bruised. Bruised apples cause rot to spread among stored fruit. Crab apples may be allowed to drop off.

Apples intended for storing should be picked just before they are ripe or they will quickly deteriorate but care must be taken not to tear the shoots when picking an unripe crop. Cooking apples may be used before they are ripe but their full flavor will develop with keeping. Apples for cider should mature on the tree. Do not leave late crops of dessert apples on the tree too late in the fall.

Storing the crop

The ideal storage place for apples is one which is cool—just below 41° F (5° C) —well-ventilated, dark and slightly moist. A loft, garage or shed is usually too dry for this purpose, but by storing the fruit in plastic bags, this problem can be overcome.

Store only sound dry fruit and do not mix varieties in one bag. Use lots of small bags so that any rot cannot spread far. After sealing them snip off a finger-nail-sized triangle from each bottom corner to ventilate. Check bags periodically and use any apples that begin to show soft bruising or brown; these apples will be inedible if left.

Exhibition tips

Apples should be picked as close as possible to the time of showing.

Pick ripe perfect fruit and leave on the stalks—all fruit is shown with the stalks in place.

Select only fruit of the same color, form and size. Uniformity can account for 25 percent of the total marks, so pay attention to these points.

Do not select the very largest fruits; those of moderate size for the variety are preferred. Perfection counts more.

Wrap each apple separately in tissue paper and pack in a box of crumpled newspaper to take them to the show. This will prevent bruising.

ICI Agricultural Division, Millbank

▲ *Effects of brown rot on fruit—the brown fruit often remains "mummified" on the tree.*

Stiff paper plates are favored for displaying fruit. Apples are never polished for shows and usually only one variety is displayed on a plate.

Pests & Diseases

Apples can be attacked by a number of pests and diseases—some of the more common are described below. A regular spraying program will keep many of them in check: scab, mildew, caterpillars eating leaves (various moths, etc.) or fruitlets (sawfly), aphids of various kinds, apple suckers, red spider mite and scale insects. American blight (woolly aphids), codling moth, canker, brown rot and bitter pit, however, may not be completely eliminated by the spray program.

Birds may do much damage to buds in winter. A netting fruit cage may be practical for small trees, otherwise, swathe trees in the rayon web sold at garden shops for the purpose.

GUIDE TO APPLE TROUBLES	
Symptoms	*Probable Causes*
Holes in fruitlets with sticky mess around them	Apple sawfly
Discolored petals on partly opened blossom buds	Apple suckers
Curling leaves and shoot tips	Aphids
Hole at eye end of fruit	Codling moth
Soft warty growth on bark	Woolly aphid
Speckled leaves	Red spider mite
Sunken, flaking bark	Canker
White powdery patches on leaves	Mildew
Brown pitting in apple flesh	Bitter pit
Fruit turning brown	Brown rot
Black or brown spots on fruit and leaves	Scab

If possible, include controls in the spray program during the tree's dormant (leafless) period. This will curb the eggs of aphids, winter moths and suckers, as well as adult scale insects. It will also clean the bark of lichen and moss which harbor troubles.

Spraying program
Each year give the tree three spray treatments. The first is when the leaves are unfolding at "green cluster" stage: captan to control scab, and malathion against aphids, apple suckers and various moth caterpillars.

The next spray, about two weeks later when the blossom buds are showing pink, contains captan and dinocap (for mildew).

The third spray is at petal fall when nearly all blossom is off. *Never spray fully opened flowers, because of the danger to bees and other pollinating insects.* This spray is against pests and diseases already mentioned, plus apple sawfly.

Pesticides can usually be applied together, *but not all are compatible,* so follow the maker's instructions.

As an alternative to a regular program of spraying you can spray only if trouble appears and cut out shoots affected by such diseases as mildew or by pests like leaf curl aphid. Regular feeding of course will do much to aid the tree's resistance to diseases and pests. Best of all, write to your state experiment station and ask for its spray chart.

Aphids: these widespread pests cause young leaves and shoot tips to curl. Leaves become sticky and sooty-looking. The insects are small, green or grey in color, and live on the underside of leaves. Remove and destroy aphids as soon as they appear and spray with an insecticide, for example, malathion.

Apple sawfly: the white maggots of apple sawfly eat into the side of fruitlets leaving a sticky mess at the entrance. The resulting apples bear ribbonlike scars. Spray with malathion when most of the flower petals have fallen.

Apple sucker: attack by this pest shows itself as waxy threads on the flower trusses leading to brown discoloration of petals and a failure to unfold. It feeds on the sap in the same way as aphids and is controlled by the same insecticides: an oil in winter, or malathion in spring.

Codling moth: the grubs of the codling moth have a brown head. From midsummer they enter the fruit near the eye and eat the center. Affected fruit becomes highly colored and drops early. Spray as recommended four weeks after petals fall and again three weeks later. To avoid this pest, tie a band of sacking around the trunk in early midsummer in which the caterpillars will pupate. Remove and burn band and cocoons in winter.

Woolly aphid: as the name suggests, this pest is covered with white fluff. It commonly feeds on the junctions of branches resulting in warty growths; the bark cracks, which allows the entry of canker and other fungal diseases. Malathion sprayed in early summer, repeated two weeks later, or brushing with methylated spirits, will control the aphids.

Red spider mite: these minute pale red insects live on the undersides of leaves and are particularly active in hot dry summers. The leaves become a speckled,

▲ *Ribbonlike scars indicate damage by the maggots of the apple sawfly.*

Step-by-step Growing Guide for Apples 23

dull, pale yellow or gray-green, wither and fall early, and new growth is stunted. Spray with derris or malathion.

Scab: this fungus disease produces black or brown spots on leaves and fruit, which later cracks and may become infected with brown rot. It is worst in a wet spring and is treated with captan. Spray at bud-bursting stage and repeat twice at 14-day intervals.

Canker: the most common fungus disease of the wood of branches, trunk and shoots, canker is especially active where soil is badly drained. The bark becomes sunken, and flakes and dies where fungus enters through tree wounds. If it encircles the stem, the branch above will die. Wherever flaking bark is seen, cut back the wood below the infection to healthy growth, making a clean cut just above a joint. Burn infected wood. Treat any large wound with a fungicidal tree wound paint.

Mildew: white powdery patches on leaves and young shoots in spring, and infected flowers which turn cream in color and do not set, are produced by mildew. Remove infected shoots and spray with an approved control.

Bitter pit: bitter pit causes small brown pits in the flesh, giving it a bitter taste.

Spray the leaves as recommended at two- to three-week intervals from early to late summer. Less hard pruning, less nitrogenous fertilizer and regular watering will keep it in check.

Brown rot: this disease infects the fruit, which turns brown then either drops, or remains mummified on the tree to infect next year's fruit. Fruit with brown skin or flesh should be destroyed as soon as seen—not stored.

Varieties

To set a crop, most apples are best if cross-pollinated. Most varieties have plenty of pollen and will pollinate one another, *provided their flowering seasons coincide or overlap.* Some have little pollen—they are known as triploid. They need a suitable pollinator to help them set their fruit, but they themselves will not pollinate the other tree. In this case there should be a third variety present (not triploid) to ensure a good crop on all three. A few varieties are self-fertile though they crop better with a suitable pollinator.

As previous mentioned there are literally hundreds of different varieties of apple. Below are some of the more readily available dessert and cooking apples, and some crab apples.

Ministry of Agriculture Food and Fisheries

▲ *An infestation of the white fluff-covered woolly aphid. Keep it under control.*

Murphy Chemicals

▲ *Symptoms of canker on a branch showing shrunken, flaking bark.*

Anoka: a summer apple highly desired for pie, applesauce, etc.; yellow-streaked red fruits of good size; hardy, often bears the year after planting.

Baldwin: an old favorite; ripens in October; large, hard, juicy and a good keeper; excellent for eating and cooking; its one drawback is a tendency toward biennial bearing unless well-thinned.

Cortland: large, beautiful, dark red fruits, fine-grained and juicy; really an improved McIntosh ripening two weeks later; excellent for cooking and eating.

Delicious: one of America's best-known apples; red, tapering, productive, it is a favorite in the Northwest for shipping East; ripens in October, keeps well.

Early McIntosh: a McIntosh hybrid, solid red, crisp and juicy; ripens early August in North; hardy, vigorous, early and reliable-bearing.

Fireside: a winter apple developed by Minnesota University; grows and fruits well in climates too cold for Delicious; fruits large, bright red over green-yellow; annual bearer, it keeps well all winter.

Golden Delicious: also a winter apple; keeps well without turning mealy; waxy-gold color; hardy and bears early.

Golden Hornet: a crab apple that is grown more for its pink-to-white blossoms and colorful fruit; can be used for jelly.

Golden Russet: a worthy successor to the old Roxbury Russet; like it, it is not colorful but it is a hard, late, good keeper; cooks well, makes excellent cider.

Hyslop: perhaps the best-known crab apple; grown for making jelly, spiced preserves, etc.; hardy, dependable, attractive.

Jonathan: bears medium-sized fruits with crisp, delicious flavor; a winter variety for cooking and eating; keeps well; a long-time favorite.

Lodi: a summer cooking sort; newer, larger-fruited, better quality than Yellow Transparent; ripens early August; vigorous, hardy, heavy-bearing.

Macoun: an improved McIntosh type; better quality, ripens later and keeps better; product of New York State Experiment Station.

McIntosh: most popular variety in Northeast; hardy, good bearer; dependable; flesh crisp and juicy—making a good cooking and eating apple; ripens September, keeps well.

A-Z Collection

⚡ The first blush of color

Pat Brindley

⚡ Golden Russet

Long Ashton Research Station

⬆ *Red Delicious*

Brian Furner

⬆ *Rhode Island Greening*

Pat Brindley

⬆ *Spigold*

George Hyde

⬆ *Golden Delicious*

Pat Brindley

⬆ *Golden Hornet (crab apple)*

Melrose: a cross between Jonathan and Delicious, it is a good late-keeping sort; firm, crisp, juicy; hardy, prolific, early-bearing; good for eating and cooking.

Northern Spy: like Baldwin and McIntosh, an old favorite; fruit large, heavily blushed and striped; hard, crisp and juicy; excellent keeper; one of the best winter apples but slow to bear.

Red Delicious: like Delicious but completely red while parent is still green; large with good aroma and flavor.

Red Dolgo: another well-known crab apple, ornamental yet good fruiter; heavy bearer; fruits small to medium, deep red; ideal pickled, in jellies and sauces.

Rhode Island Greening: an old-time apple, long a favorite for pies, sauces, cooked desserts; tree vigorous and productive; keeps well in storage.

Rome Beauty: large-fruited apple of good quality; deep red, thick-skinned—stands handling; bears early.

Spigold: another New York State introduction—a cross between Northern Spy and Delicious; fruits large, marbled with red; vigorous, very early-bearing; mid to late October; very promising.

Stark Earliest: one of the very earliest apples; good rich color; flavor and quality good; prolific and dependable bearer.

Starkrimson Delicious: fall-fruiting; starts bearing early; an early-reddening, superior Delicious-type; successful over a wide area.

Stayman Winesap: a favorite in middle belt and upper South especially; large, crisp, fine-grained with spicy flavor; vigorous, bears well and early.

Wealthy: an old favorite fall apple; trouble-free, dependable; good for cooking and baking if picked early—pick fully ripe for eating; keeps well.

Williams Red: looks like Delicious but a darker red with faint stripings; flesh is pure white and juicy; ripens early in August.

Yellow Transparent: an old apple that ripens in July or early August; fruit of good size, skin clear white to pale yellow; excellent flavor for early apple; fine for pies, sauces, etc.; upright, hardy, early-bearing.

York-A-Red: not so well known as some but a good winter sort for eating and for making cider, fair cooking; hardy and keeps well.

▲ *Ready for picking*

▲ *Grimes Golden*

Apricots

Prunus armeniaca (fam. *Rosaceae*)
Hardy deciduous tree with a useful life
of 10–20 years
Planting to harvesting time: 2–3 years.
Size: 15 × 15 ft (4.5 × 4.5 m); 8–12 × 15 ft (2.4–3.6 × 4.5 m)
as a fan
Yield: about 44 lb (20 kg) for a fan or mature, semidwarf
tree

This luxurious orange-fleshed fruit is almost as luscious as the peach, and some connoisseurs prefer its slightly tangy flavor and juicy sweetness to that of its near relative. Apricots grow on small and ornamental trees, and are therefore a very good choice for the gardener, especially if shelter from early spring frosts can be provided for the white or pale pink flowers.

There are two other species of prunus which provide apricotlike fruits: the Japanese apricot, *P. mume,* is one of them. It has small and not very well flavored fruit, and is grown much more for its attractive appearance, since it produces single, pink, almond-scented flowers in profusion in spring. The other species is *P. x dasycarpa,* the black apricot, grown for a similar reason, since the shoots are purple, and a cloud of white flowers is produced in early spring. The fruits are black with a purple bloom, about 1½ in (4 cm) wide, with the typical apricot flavor, but are seldom, if ever, seen.

The apricot was probably introduced to the West some time during the six-teenth century, but it took perhaps another two hundred years for it to become a popular and widely-grown fruit.

Apricots are grown in large quantities commercially in the warmer climates, such as those of the Pacific Coast, Mediterranean seaboard, and in Australia. However, there is no reason why they should not do as well in a temperate climate as the peach does, and produce satisfactory crops in most seasons.

Choosing the tree

Apricot trees, as with other fruit trees, usually consist of a scion budded onto a rootstock which influences the vigor and final height of the tree.

You can grow apricots from the stones, but as these are "seedlings," their cropping potential will vary, and they will come into fruit some years after budded trees. When you buy an apricot from a nursery, choose a one- or two-year-old scion.

Apricots can be trained as spur-pruned cordons, but since apricot crops tend to be rather small, because the trees

▲ *Juicy sweet apricots taste as good as they look. The trees, too, are decorative.*

fruit better if not too tightly pruned, this form should only be used where space is very limited.

Suitable site and soil
The apricot, like the peach, is a fruit that needs warmth in summer to do really well, though, also like the peach, it must have cool winters in order to rest and become completely dormant. It can be grown as a tree in the open, and in a formal shape, usually a fan, trained flat against a wall.

Whatever site you choose for it, the apricot should not be planted in a frost pocket, or where it is exposed to wind,

Step-by-step Growing Guide for Apricots

PREPARATION

1. Dig a hole at least two spits deep and add organic matter for a trained tree.

2. Erect training wires 6 in (15 cm) apart using vine eyes or similar supports.

even if the prevailing wind is a southwest one. Shelter is required, both to make sure that any pollinating insects which are about at the time when the flowers open are not discouraged, and to give the fruit every chance to ripen fully.

Having given your tree the best possible site, you should make certain that the soil in which it is to spend its life is as near perfectly suited to its needs as can be managed, especially as the apricot is rather temperamental about its root environment. If your garden soil naturally consists of a deep—preferably 3 ft (90 cm)—not very acid loam, you should be able to obtain consistently good crops of fruit from healthy and vigorous trees.

Well drained soils containing a lot of sand will tend to be too dry and short of plant food, but can be improved before planting by giving extra quantities of bulky organic matter, and by giving heavier mulches of the same material during the tree's life. Greater quantities of plant food will also be needed.

Badly drained, heavy soils, especially those with a clay subsoil, should not be planted to apricots, unless you are determined to grow them. In that case, conditions can be somewhat ameliorated by digging out the soil to a depth of 2 ft (60 cm) and mixing rubble or broken brick into the bottom of the hole, then return-

ing the soil liberally laced with a light loam, coarse sand, peat or grit. Since the tree's roots will spread considerably, it is a good idea to treat as large an area as convenient or possible.

Soil preparation
The average soil, which shows no very marked characteristics of good or bad drainage, should be prepared some weeks in advance of planting, by digging to a depth of at least two spits, forking up the bottom of the hole, and returning the soil, mixed with rotted organic matter such as garden compost, farm manure, leafmold or similar material, at the rate of a 2–2½ gal (10–12 L) bucket per sq yd (sq m). The apricot likes a slightly limy soil, so add lime to bring the pH up to neutral (7.0 +) or nearly so.

A few days before planting, bonemeal can be added at 4 oz per sq yd (120 g per sq m). Sprinkle it evenly over the surface where the tree is to be planted and rake or water it in.

Planting
The best time to plant the apricot is as early in spring as possible because it starts into growth so early. If planting from a container, do it very carefully.

If you are planning to grow a fan-trained tree on a dwarfing stock against a

PLANTING

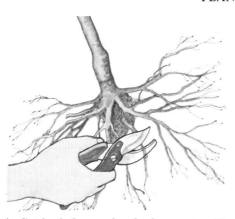

1. Cut back damaged or broken roots with shears.

2. If the roots are dry, soak them in a bucket of tepid water.

3. Plant the tree with the soil mark just at the soil level. Leave the soil in a slight mound and rake the surface to make it porous. Then tie the tree to the wires.

wall, allow it a length of wall 15 ft (4.5 m) long and about 8 ft (2.4 m) high, and plant 6 in (15 cm) away from the wall. A number of trees should be spaced 10 ft (3 m) apart. They will overlap but the ends of the shoots can be headed back towards their own trunk if need be. Trees on more vigorous rootstocks will need to be 20 ft (6 m) apart.

Plant the tree so that the uppermost roots are about 3 in (7.5 cm) below the soil surface, and make sure that the hole is large enough to take the roots spread out to their fullest extent. If any roots are broken or torn, cut them back cleanly to just behind the damage. If they became at all dry during transit, soak them for an hour or two in a bucket of tepid water before planting.

Once in the planting hole, cover the roots with a layer of crumbled soil, shake the tree a little to settle the soil around them, and then fill in the hole gradually, firming as you go.

Finish off by raking the surface so that it is not smooth and impervious to the entry of moisture and air. You can, if you like, put a light mulch of leafmold or garden compost around the newly planted tree.

Since fan-shaped trees are trained spread flat against a wall, it will be nec-

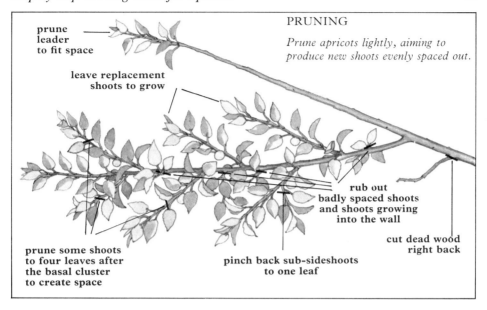

prune leader to fit space

leave replacement shoots to grow

PRUNING

Prune apricots lightly, aiming to produce new shoots evenly spaced out.

rub out badly spaced shoots and shoots growing into the wall

cut dead wood right back

prune some shoots to four leaves after the basal cluster to create space

pinch back sub-sideshoots to one leaf

essary to supply wires to which the shoots and branches can be tied. These wires should be spaced 6–9 in (15–22.5 cm) apart, with the lowest one 1 ft (30 cm) from the ground, and can be secured with vine eyes so that the wires are held 4 in (10 cm) away from the wall.

Trees in the open may need staking in the first few years of their life and the stake should be put in position before the tree is planted.

Training a fan-shaped tree
The initial training of a fan-shaped tree is the same as for peaches, though you will find that apricots do not produce such luxuriant growth and training them will be less time consuming and less complicated. Once the main ribs of the fan are established, which will take two to three years, depending on the age of the tree when you start, maintenance pruning each year will be necessary.

Your aim in pruning is to encourage the tree to produce new shoots, evenly spaced out, regularly every year. This is achieved by pruning the right amount at the right time, but you should also make sure that sufficient growth is left untouched, so that it can produce buds and fruit. Too hard pruning will give too much vegetative growth; too little or no pruning at all will result in a sequence of heavy crops, which may exhaust the tree and give poor quality fruit, as well as small crops.

Although the apricot will fruit on one-year-old shoots, it carries more and better quality fruit on growth which is two or three years old. There is no need to do the extensive cutting out, rubbing and pinching back helpful with the peach, though the principles which are followed are roughly the same. Remember, however, that hard pruning results in a smaller crop, and it is better to prune the apricot comparatively lightly.

The considerable risk of infection by dieback means that the safest time to prune is in early spring. Unavoidably, some pruning has to be done later than this, but it should be kept to a minimum.

As with the peach, any new shoots which grow directly into the wall or directly away from it, should be rubbed out as soon as they become obvious. Any weak new shoots should be removed, and also those which have died back from the tip; cut these back to living growth or remove them altogether.

Then, two or three weeks later when the remaining new shoots have grown somewhat, the best of these should be earmarked to form replacement branches and tied in so that they are evenly spaced between the current main growths. They can be allowed to grow without being stopped throughout the season, and should be spaced at least 1 ft (30 cm) apart.

Of the remainder, some can be completely removed, and some can be stopped after the fourth leaf beyond the cluster of leaves at the base. If the shoots that are not removed then produce sub-sideshoots during the season, again they can either be completely removed, or pinched back to one leaf beyond the basal cluster, when they have grown to about three leaves long.

Some very strong shoots will probably be produced in the center of the fan; these should be cut out completely unless they are needed as replacement shoots. Since the best crops are produced on two- and three-year-old shoots and spurs, it is wise to remove periodically the oldest growth every five or six years. This will mean cutting out one or two branches of the framework of the fan, and so a similar number of strong new shoots should be retained and tied in to take their place. Do not prune or pinch back these replacement shoots.

If in doubt whether to prune out or pinch back a shoot, leave it alone, provided the growth is not too crowded. Light rather than heavy pruning of apricots will give you the heaviest crops.

In autumn, cut off the growing points of the leading shoots, and those side-shoots which have been kept for future replacements. Also remove the oldest spurs completely.

Pruning a bush tree

If you consider that a conventional tree will fruit satisfactorily in your garden, the pruning should aim at building up an open-centered framework of primary branches, on which the fruiting side-shoots will be carried. The subsequent pruning should be light, but aimed at helping the tree produce new shoots every year, spaced evenly over the tree.

Prune before growth starts in the spring, and in general follow the instructions for pruning a bush peach.

Flowering and pollination

The apricot is self-fertile and does not need another variety to cross-pollinate it. It flowers in early spring, or sometimes even earlier if it is grown on a wall. Hence, where there is a great risk of frost damage to the blossoms, protection should be supplied in the form of cloth or clear plastic sheeting draped over the tree, hung from wires or wooden battens, and rolled back during the day when the weather is warmer. Be careful to see that the protective covering does not touch the flowers.

In the early spring, especially if cool, there may be few pollinating insects about, and you may have to do some

Use a child's paintbrush to transfer pollen from one flower to another to obtain a good fruit set.

hand pollination to get a good fruit set. When the flowers are fully open, which is usually at midday, transfer the pollen from one flower to another with the help of a child's paintbrush, stroking it lightly over the center of each flower.

Watering

Apricots come from regions which have hot summers and little rain; what rain does occur during the growing season is mostly very heavy, but of short duration. The soil at the foot of a wall tends to be drier than that in the rest of the garden, which will suit the apricot well, but it will still need an occasional good watering, especially when the fruit is about the size of a marble. Lack of moisture at this time could mean that the natural fruit drop is heavier than usual and a poor crop results.

If dry weather follows planting, supply the young tree with moisture. If it runs short at a time when it is so vulner-

CARE AND CULTIVATION

1. In the late winter, add 10-10-10 at 1 oz per sq yd (30 g per sq m).

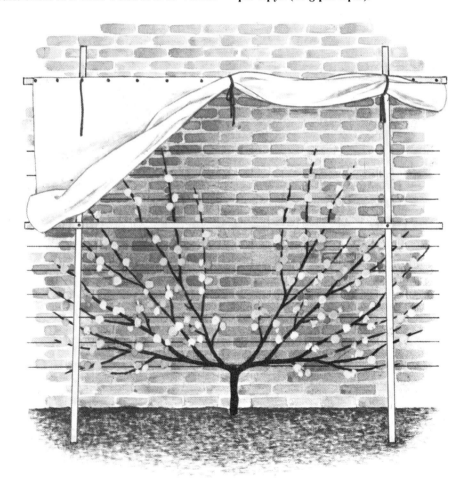

2. Apricots flower in early spring. If there is great risk of frost damaging the blossoms, protect the tree with a cover hung from the wooden battens.

CARE OF THE FRUIT

1. First remove small and misshapen fruit. Then thin so that there is only one fruit per cluster.

2. Protect the ripening fruit against birds and wasps with some perforated plastic bags.

able, it is liable to die. When you do water, give a good soaking with a sprinkler attachment to the hose, leaving it running so that it wets the soil down several inches.

Make sure that the tree always has reserves of moisture to call on in the soil; irregular supplies of water can result in poor fruit set, fruit drop and fruit split, as well as stone cracking.

Feeding
Like the plum, the main need of apricots is for nitrogen, and in acid soils they also require lime. You can give the trees

10-10-10 or, if an added push is needed, use sulfate ammonia at the rate of 1 oz per sq yd (30 g per sq m). In that case, however, you should give them ground limestone every four years or so, to maintain the pH at the correct value. In any case, it is a good idea to test the soil periodically for the pH value, to be sure that it is sufficiently limy but not becoming extremely so, which would cause the fruit trees to suffer from lime-induced chlorosis.

If growth becomes overly vigorous, it can be slowed down by the addition of potassium at the same time of year, using either sulfate of potash at 1 oz per sq yd (30 g per sq m), or wood ashes at about 5 oz per sq yd (150 g per sq m).

All these fertilizers should be sprinkled evenly around the tree, remembering that the roots will spread at least as far underground as the branches extend above it.

In late spring a top dressing of rotted organic matter, such as farm manure, spent mushroom soil, leafmold or garden compost, can be spread around the tree to cover the border, about 1 in (2.5 cm) deep. This will maintain the soil structure, keep the weeds down, and prevent the evaporation of moisture.

A further, though not essential, dressing of this kind can be given in autumn after the fruit has been picked, and any that remains in late winter should be forked in carefully before fertilizer is applied.

Care of the fruit
Provided frost has not been a problem, the apricot sets a good crop of fruit, and more often than not will need thinning. A natural fruit drop will occur and when you have seen how much fruit remains, start thinning if it seems necessary. By this time the fruit should be about the size of a marble.

First remove those fruits that are injured, misshapen or small, and then thin every pair or cluster of fruit so that only one remains. Finally remove enough to make sure that the remainder are spaced about 5 in (12.5 cm) apart.

R. J. Corbin

▲ Apricots produce several fruits on each cluster but will do better if you thin to only one.

Some of the thinning can be done after the natural fruit drop, the remainder after the stoning has been completed. You will be able to determine this stage because while stoning is occurring the fruit ceases to swell. When it is complete, swelling starts again and it is then that thinning can be finished.

As the fruits increase in size, it is helpful to the final coloring and ripening of the fruits if leaves and shoots which shade them from the sun are removed. You may find that birds and wasps begin to attack from midsummer, so cover the fruit with perforated plastic bags if needed.

Harvesting
The earliest varieties become ripe in midsummer, and picking from the later ones will continue through late summer, possibly into early autumn. Do not pick the fruits as soon as they have reached their full color and have stopped swelling. Although the flesh may be soft, they will be somewhat lacking in the typical

sharp apricot flavor. It is better to wait a few days more to give the fruit time to develop to full maturity.

If the season is one which is particularly troubled with wasps, you can pick a little early but leave the fruit in the sun for a few hours and then bring them in for a day or two before eating.

Be careful when picking, as the stalk is easily torn away from the fruit.

Apricots make excellent pot trees.

Growing apricots in containers

If for some reason you cannot grow a tree in the soil, either because of lack of room or because any suitable areas are paved or concreted, good trees can be grown in large pots or tubs. There is the added advantage with this method of growing that the trees are mobile, and you can put them under cover during the spring frosts and so make sure of getting good crops, as well as being able to protect them fully in other severe weather.

Choose a container of at least 12 in (30 cm) diameter, big enough to take the tree roots comfortably without being cramped and doubled up. Put a layer of drainage material in the bottom, such as crock, small pieces of brick, gravel and so on, to a depth of about 1 in (2.5 cm), and then fill in with a little of a good potting soil. Set the tree in this, spreading the roots out, and fill in with more soil, occasionally shaking the plant a little, so that the soil settles well around the roots.

When potting is complete, the surface of the soil should be level with the soil mark on the trunk of the tree, but remember also that a space of about 1 in (2.5 cm) deep should be left between the surface and the pot rim, to allow for watering.

The potting soil needs to be thoroughly and evenly firmed in, especially at the sides, and when potting is finished, the plant should be watered. Then it should be put in a sheltered place while it becomes established, at the same time keeping an eye on its water needs.

If you can plunge the container into soil in a sheltered place during the winter, this will protect the roots from frost. Otherwise cover the container well with sacking, straw, or fiberglass wool.

Pruning an apricot in a container is done so as to encourage it to form a pyramid shape. Prune the leader in early spring in the first two or three years, and pinch back sideshoots, if needed, in summer, so that they are quite short and form spurs in due course. Although this is contrary to normal pruning techniques, apricots in containers tend to be very fruitful, partly because their roots are restricted, and the method works well. Very strong rank-growing shoots should be removed completely.

Never allow the plants to run short of water, and give a general slow acting complete fertilizer in spring. Water this well in; the quantity should be about 2 oz (60 g) per tree. A top dressing of rotted garden compost or leafmold in late spring may also be useful.

Transplanting into slightly larger containers, up to a maximum of about 16–

Step-by-step Growing Guide for Apricots

18 in (40–45 cm) diameter, will be needed every year. Replace some of the old soil from the outside of the root ball with fresh material.

Otherwise care of the tree is as for the normally grown specimens.

Do not expect a container grown apricot to live as long as the open-ground ones. However, you should get useful crops for about seven or eight years from the time it comes into cropping.

Exhibition tips

Apricots are one of the more suitable fruits for exhibition, as they ripen from midsummer onwards, and by careful choice of variety it will be possible to have fruit ready for a summer or autumn show. Points are awarded for condition, color, size and uniformity.

First class thinning will go a long way to helping you win an award, so you should allow much more space between fruit, in order that they will become large. A spacing of 8 in (20 cm) is not too much; you should make sure that they get all the sun and air possible by removing overhanging leaves and turning the fruit towards the light.

Be very careful with watering, and, as the fruit gets near to ripening, take precautions against wasps and birds by net-

▲ *Moorpark*

ting the tree, or place clear perforated plastic bags over individual fruits.

For one exhibit you may need a dish of nine fruits of one variety only, unless the schedule allows mixed dishes. Pick the apricots as late as possible, so that they are really fresh and smooth skinned and handle them as little as possible to retain the bloom. Be careful not to tear the stalk or fruit when picking. Choose fruit without blemishes, all as nearly the same in size and color as possible, and typical of the variety concerned.

Stage them on a plate, evenly spaced with one or two in the center and the remainder arranged round them. They should be placed with the stalk end underneath.

Varieties

Aprigold: compact grower suitable for patio tub; fruit yellow, flavorful. Attractive blossoms; self-fertile.

Earli-Orange: orange-fleshed freestone. Ripen on tree. Eat fresh, canned, frozen or dried. Late June-July.

Early Golden: highly flavored freestone; medium-sized, smooth skin, pale orange.

Goldcot: large, orange-yellow with red cheek; productive, freestone. August.

▲ *Red-flushed apricots are extremely attractive and very suitable for exhibition.*

Step-by-step Growing Guide for Apricots

Moongold: fruits medium-sized, pale gold, sweet, orange flesh; disease-free, vigorous. From Minnesota; mid-July.

Moorpark: old but good; tasty freestone. Deep yellow with red cheek. Blooms late, ripens July.

Nugget: very productive, consistent cropper. Fruits attractive, richly flavored; June–July.

Sungold: round, gold with orange blush; orange flesh, tender, mild. Tree upright, ripens late July.

Tilton: fruit large, oval, orange; tree vigorous, prolific. More drought-resistant than most; not for coastal California.

Wilson Delicious: very hardy, prolific, reliable; fruit large, well-flavored. Good canner, freezer. Early to mid-July.

Pests & Diseases

Red spider mite: it can be a problem on outdoor trees, especially if trained against walls. The leaves of infected trees become mottled with tiny gray or yellow specks and the minute red insects can be seen underneath. In bad attacks webbing will be produced on the leaves and stems.

The pest flourishes in dry, hot conditions, so spray the tree frequently with a hard stream of water if you have had previous attacks of this pest. Spray with an approved miticide as needed.

Scale insects: these sap sucking insects can sometimes be spotted by the mold which grows on the sticky substance (honeydew) which they secrete. Both the leaves and stems of the trees may be covered with the sticky black mold. If you look more closely at the bark and under-surfaces of the leaves you should also be able to see the small, brown, round or oval raised spots which are the insects.

Scale insects are best controlled by a dormant oil spray which attacks the hi-

▲ Aphids suck the sap, particularly from the young leaves.

bernating eggs. If, despite this, the insects appear in the summer, spray with malathion.

Aphids: these sucking insect pests feed by sucking the sap from the leaves, particularly at the tips of the new shoots. They also attack the soft young stems, and growth in spring and summer will be checked, sometimes severely, with the leaves being curled and discolored yellow or pale green. Such an attack can open the way to infestation by the dieback fungus.

Dieback (Blossom wilt): this is a serious disease of apricots and has often been blamed for the decline in the frequency with which they have been grown. It is a fungal disease but often appears to attack if the tree has been damaged by too severe pruning or by winter frosts. Bad soil drainage predisposes the tree to infection; some varieties are more prone to it than others.

To begin with, the disease attacks the tips of the young shoots (and blossom if present) but then moves back along the branch slowly killing the whole branch. The leaves turn brown and fall prematurely; the bark of the shoots turns brown, and no new growth is produced on that part of the shoot. Gum may also be produced on the larger branches.

Step-by-step Growing Guide for Apricots 39

▲ An early symptom of fungus disease is evident on the leaves.

▲ Brown rot attacks the fruit, normally entering through wounds.

Cut dead shoots and branches right back to healthy wood, in late spring, when general pruning is started. Then paint over the cut surface of the larger wounds at once with a wound sealing compound.

Brown rot: this fungus attacks the fruit, normally entering through wounds caused by birds, caterpillars or other insects. Infected fruits quickly turn soft and brown and become covered with concentric circles of buff-colored fungus. The disease can spread through all the fruits in a cluster or store by contact between fruits. As soon as you see a diseased fruit, whether on the ground, on the tree or in storage, remove it and burn it. The fungus can also travel from the fruit to the fruiting spur and can cause dieback, so cut out and burn the adjacent spur as well.

Japanese and other beetles: attack leaves or fruits, eating holes. When present, spray promptly with Sevin or malathion.

Canker worms and caterpillars: various kinds may attack. Control by spraying with Sevin or malathion as needed.

Curculio: beetles lay eggs in the young fruits causing "worms" in apples and all stone fruits. In home garden, spray with malathion or the combination spray recommended for apples by your state authorities when the petals fall. Repeat 10 days later and again 14 days after that.

Peach tree borer: these tunnel into trunk at or near ground line. Traditional advice is to place a ring of moth flakes one inch from the trunk and cover with soil in the spring. Alternatively, spray the lower trunk with the current material recommended by your state experiment station.

GUIDE TO APRICOT TROUBLES	
Symptoms	*Probable cause*
Yellow orange-speckled leaves, premature leaf fall, webbing on leaves and stems	Red spider mite
Clear sticky substance on leaves, sometimes black patches, raised brown spots on bark and leaves	Scale insect
Curled young leaves and shoots, growth stops	Aphids
New shoots and leaves brown from tip	Dieback
Fruit with brown patches becoming soft, sometimes beige colored pustules on patches	Brown rot

Globe Artichokes

Cynara scolymus (fam. *Compositae*)
Hardy perennial with a useful life of four to five years
Planting to harvesting time: plants crop in the second year from offsets, in the third year from seed
Size: the bushy, herbaceous plants reach 3–5 ft (90–150 cm) high, 44 in (1 m) in diameter; immature flower heads eaten when about 4 in (10 cm) long
Yield: 24–48 heads or buds per plant per season under favorable conditions

The globe artichoke is a strikingly handsome, very large, thistlelike plant which is as decorative as it is delicious. The part of the plant which is eaten is the immature flower bud or "choke." These are produced over several months, from midsummer through midautumn, or even later in exceptionally mild weather. The buds are harvested and cooked; at the table the petallike scales are removed one by one, and the fleshy base of each eaten. The succulent flat, platelike structure at the bottom of the flower is eaten last; this bit is called the heart (botanically, it is the receptacle of the flower) and is considered a real delicacy.

Globe artichokes are native to Europe and widely grown there, particularly in the warmer Mediterranean areas. They were planted in Louisiana by French settlers and in California by the Spaniards, and also cultivated by early settlers in Florida. They are very easy to grow in a mild climate and commercially are grown almost exclusively along the central California coast. They can be grown in southern states and, with care, as far north as Long Island, New York. For a minimum outlay, you can have a steady supply of this unusual vegetable every summer. One word of advice: globe artichokes are not completely frost-hardy and need protection during the worst periods of winter cold. If you live in the colder northern states, or your garden is very exposed, it is best to forego planting globe artichokes, as you are likely to be disappointed.

Although perennial, it is a short-lived plant in cool temperate climates, and needs replacing after three to five years of cropping. As it sends up numerous rooted suckers, replacement from your own stock is an easy operation.

Each plant takes up quite a bit of space; however, its large, pale gray arching leaves are so attractive that a few artichoke plants can be put among shrubs or in the herbaceous border if you are short of room in the vegetable garden.

Pat Brindley

▲ *The immature flower buds, or "chokes" of globe artichokes; these are ready for harvesting.*

Although flower buds left to reach maturity and bloom are inedible, the bluish purple thistles are very attractive, and are highly prized by flower arrangers. Varieties with purple, rather than green, flower buds can be obtained abroad. However, although these are particularly decorative, many people consider them less tasty than the more common, green artichokes.

Suitable site and soil
The ideal position is sunny, well protected from wind and away from trees and hedges. If you are planning your kitchen garden on a rotation system, remember that artichokes normally remain where they are planted for at least four years, and will eventually develop into large, spreading plants. Each plant will need 4 ft × 4 ft (1.2 m × 1.2 m) of room, and this limits the number of artichoke plants you can grow in a small garden. They can reach an ultimate height of 5 ft (1.5 m), so avoid siting them where they overshadow smaller plants. Frost pockets and low lying sites are unsuitable, as artichokes will fail to crop in these conditions.

Globe artichokes are heavy feeders

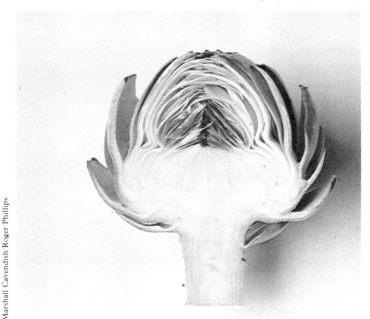

◄A cross section through an immature artichoke flower. The fleshy tissue at the base of each petallike scale is eaten. When all the leaves have been removed, the flat, succulent, platelike structure at the base of the flower is eaten. This portion, called the heart, is considered the most delicious.

Marshall Cavendish Roger Phillips

and like a light rich soil which is moisture retentive but well drained; avoid waterlogged soils. These plants will give several years of good crops only if they have a deep bed, rich in nutrients. If you have a heavy soil, double dig it, breaking up the subsoil; lighten the top soil with ashes, coarse sand, peat or grit. All soils should have plenty of well-rotted manure incorporated into them before planting. If you can get it, composted seaweed is a very good alternative to manure; in nature, relatives of globe artichokes are found growing wild by the sea. Dig manure or compost in well before planting, in late winter or early spring, at a rate of about half a barrow-load per 6 sq yd (5 sq m). A complete fertilizer should also be incorporated into the soil about ten days before planting, at the rate of 3 oz per sq yd (100 g per sq m). Do not simply sprinkle it on the surface of the soil; fork it in thoroughly. Bonemeal, at the rate of 1 lb per sq yd (450 g per sq m) can be dug in at the same time and, as it is a slow acting fertilizer, will continue to provide phosphorus for the extensive root system over a long period of time. Lastly, make sure the soil is absolutely free of perennial weeds, because few garden jobs are as painful or difficult as weeding between large, prickly artichoke plants.

Sowing and planting

Artichokes can be grown from seed but, although initially less expensive than buying rooted suckers, this does have disadvantages. The main drawback is that plants raised from seed do not necessarily have any of the good qualities of the parent plant, and many of the seedlings will be inferior croppers. Secondly, there will be a longer time span between sowing and the first crops, and valuable space in your garden will be temporarily nonproductive.

If you wish to grow the plants from seed, start them in a heated greenhouse or in the home in late winter. When the seedlings are large enough to handle, prick them out into 3 in (7.5 cm) pots. In midspring, begin to harden the young plants in a cold frame, and, when thoroughly hardened, plant them out in late spring, by which time the weather should have warmed up. In the nursery bed, they can be planted quite closely to-

Step-by-step Growing Guide for Artichokes

PLANTING AND CULTIVATION

1. Plant rooted offsets in mid- to late spring; space them 3–4 ft (90–120 cm) apart, with 4 ft (1.2 m) between rows.

2. In spring, sprinkle nitrate of soda at the rate of ½ oz (15 g) per plant; do this when the soil is damp.

3. Make sure the artichokes get plenty of water through spring and summer, particularly when the weather is dry.

4. To support tall-growing plants, tie main stem to a strong stake inserted deeply into the soil.

gether, say 6–9 in (15–22.5 cm) apart. In mid- to late summer, these young plants will probably form flower buds; retain the most promising plants and dig up and put the remainder on the compost heap. Remove the flower buds from the chosen plants, if you wish them to be really strong croppers in future. The following midspring, plant them out in their final position, spaced 4 ft (1.2 m) apart.

Alternatively, sow the seeds outdoors, after the last spring frost. Make the drills ½ in (1.3 cm) deep and 1 ft (30 cm) apart. Thin the seedlings to 6 in (15 cm) apart, to avoid overcrowding. Outdoor sown seeds are unlikely to form flower heads during the first summer, so the selection process is delayed for a whole year.

A far safer method, though slightly more expensive, is to buy offsets. If you already have an established bed you can easily propagate new plants from off-shoots produced by your own plants. Vegetative propagation makes certain that all of the good qualities of the par-

HARVESTING

1. If any flower buds form in the first year of planting, remove them as soon as they are seen.

2. From the second year onward, pick the king heads first, when they are about 4 in (10 cm) in diameter.

3. To store surplus artichokes, cut them with 1 ft (30 cm) of stalk, and push the stems into damp sand.

ent plant will be present in the young plants. Buy the offsets in midspring, or late spring in cold areas, and plant them out immediately. Plant firmly in trowel holes, 4 in (10 cm) deep, in rows 4 ft (1.2 m) apart, with 3–4 ft (90–120 cm) between plants. The growing points should just be visible above the soil. Shade them with temporary screening from bright sun for a month or so, until established, and keep them well watered.

Cultivation and care
Artichokes need plenty of water through spring and summer, particularly in dry weather; never allow them to become dry at the roots. In spring, sprinkle nitrate of soda, at the rate of ½ oz (15 g) per plant, onto damp soil; this gives the plants a good start for the growing season. On clay soils substitute sulfate of ammonia for nitrate of soda, as the salts in the latter make heavy soils even stickier.

In summer, apply a good liquid fertilizer at ten day intervals; one or two weak doses of chelated iron (marketed under several names) applied when growth is most vigorous is a particularly beneficial treatment if the plants are growing on a limestone soil. Lawn mowings spread around the plants from time to time help to retain soil moisture and also keep weeds down. If weeds are particularly troublesome, hoeing may be necessary. Healthy plants normally produce many more suckers than are needed; in early summer remove all but the five strongest from the base.

Tall plants, or those growing in exposed positions, may need staking. Choose stakes firm enough to bear the full weight of the plant and insert them firmly into the soil. Tie the main stem to the stake, allowing room for the plant to sway naturally; otherwise, the stem may snap in strong winds.

Harvesting
Newly planted artichokes should not be allowed to crop the first year after planting. Some small flower buds may appear during the first summer, and these

Bernard Alfieri

▲ *A fully mature artichoke in flower; though attractive, at this stage they are inedible.*

should be pinched out as soon as they are seen. This allows the young plant to channel its energy into the development of strong, healthy roots, which will in turn lead to heavier future crops.

In the second summer after planting, large terminal buds, known as "king heads" will form. If you are aiming for fewer but larger heads, then cut off the smaller lateral buds which surround the king head. If you wait until these lateral buds are about 2 in (5 cm) long, you can eat them either raw, pickled, or fried. Alternatively, if it is quantity rather than quality and size that you require, leave the lateral buds on the plant to develop fully. By removing the king head, even more lateral buds will form, which can then be bottled in oil.

In some parts of the South and Southwest, the season is reversed and harvesting is done between November and June. In July, the old plants are cut back.

Pick the king heads first, when they are about 4 in (10 cm) in diameter, leaving about 6 in (15 cm) of stalk attached. It is most important to harvest this crop at exactly the right moment; if you leave it slightly too long, all will be lost. A head ready for picking will have green,

tightly packed leaves which should not be starting to open for flowering. No blue-purple thistle should be showing at the top. The immature but ripe-for-eating artichoke is smaller than the full grown artichoke, but the latter is absolutely inedible.

Each plant should produce five or more king heads. Once the king heads are picked, more sideshoots develop and smaller heads will grow on these, thus extending the season of cropping.

If you are faced with a sudden glut of artichokes ready for picking, do not leave them on the plant to go to seed. If you cut them with about 1 ft (30 cm) of stalk attached and push the stems into damp sand, they will keep for about a week.

Care after harvesting

After all the good heads have been gathered, cut down the stems to ground level. Winter protection for the crowns depends on the location of your garden. In very mild areas, cutting back the leaves by half, and then tying the remainder firmly together is adequate protection. In most places, more protection will be necessary if the plants are not to die com-

PROPAGATION

1. Take offsets from established plants in midautumn or midspring; make sure there is plenty of root attached.

2. Protect autumn-planted offsets with plastic covers, or pot them up and put them in a cold frame.

pletely. In late autumn, mulch well with a non-packing material. In most areas the usual mulches can cause rotting of the plants if the winter should prove damp, as it often does in the South.

Although artichokes are not particularly frost hardy, too much winter protection can do more harm than good. If the plants are covered too long, they will make early, soft, lush growth which will quickly succumb to any late spring frosts. Remove the coverings in early to mid spring. It is better to do this, replacing the protection if there is a late frost, rather than leave it on until all danger of frost has passed. No row should be left to grow after it is more than four years old. Plant a new row of offsets each year, so the old rows can be dug up and replaced.

Propagation
Once you have an established bed of globe artichokes, you can easily detach the rooted suckers, or offsets, from the base of the parent plant and grow them on as replacements. Ideally, to have a continual, uninterrupted supply, this should be done during the second cropping season of the existing bed. The young offsets will begin cropping in the second summer after detaching, in the season directly following the one in

which the parent plants finished their productive life and were consigned to the compost heap. Whenever you decide to propagate globe artichokes, remember that it takes fifteen to nineteen months from the time the offsets are detached until they begin cropping.

Offsets can be taken in mid- or late autumn, or else in midspring. If you live in a mild area, autumn is probably the best time as the plants will be well settled in before spring. In cold or exposed areas, wait until the weather has warmed up in spring. The process of detaching the offsets from the parent plant is very simple. With a trowel, scrape away the soil until you can see where the offset is joined to the old plant. Then use a sharp knife to sever the offset, making sure there is a bit of the old stock attached and plenty of fine roots. Offsets 10 in (25 cm) high are the safest ones to select, as they are most likely to recover from the shock of transplanting without ill effects.

Once they have been severed, they should be replanted as soon as possible.

Blanched chards
When a plant has come to the end of its cropping life, and you intend to replace it with a young rooted cutting, it can be

Step-by-step Growing Guide for Artichokes

made to produce a single crop of blanched shoots, called "chards" in autumn. These tender, succulent shoots are cooked like cardoons or Swiss chard and can be obtained for a minimum of effort.

In midsummer, when flower head production has ceased, cut back the leaves to within 6 in (15 cm) of the ground and cut the stems back to ground level. Water the plants weekly until the beginning of midautumn. What you are after is a quick crop of strong new leaves, because once blanching begins, no new growth is made. When the young leaves are 2 ft (60 cm) high, tie them firmly together with soft twine or raffia. Next, wrap brown paper around and over them, or cover them over with clean dry straw. Lastly, earth-up the whole lot with fine ashes or sifted soil, so that all light is excluded.

Blanching should be finished in five to six weeks. If you still have some fully blanched chards left in the garden when cold weather sets in, lift and store them in boxes filled with dry sand.

Exhibition tips
Globe artichokes are at their best at the height of the show season, and if well grown can be an attractive addition to a collection of vegetables, or shown on their own as a single dish. In both categories, six artichokes is the usual number shown.

There is no special timing called for, as the plants continue to produce a series of flower heads on the lateral branches throughout the summer and early autumn period. The king heads formed early in the season on the end of the central stems are usually larger than those produced on the side branches, but adequate heads can usually be found lower down the plant.

Try to pick the artichokes as close to the show time as possible. If you have to pick them a few days earlier, cut the heads with about 1 ft (30 cm) of stalk attached. Then put the stems in a bucket or other deep container full of water. Change the water every other day and at the same time trim the bottom 1 in

BLANCHED CHARDS

1. **In autumn, when leaves are 2 ft (60 cm) high, tie them firmly together with soft twine or raffia.**

2. **Wrap brown corrugated paper around them, or, alternatively, cover them with plenty of clean, dry straw.**

3. **Lastly, earth up the whole lot with sifted soil or fine ashes, so that all light is excluded from the shoots.**

➤ *The gray-green, deeply cut leaves of the artichoke plant are very handsome, and they can be grown equally well in the flower garden or vegetable plot. Remember that once established, artichokes grow vigorously and quite tall, so keep them away from smaller-growing plants.*

Marshall Cavendish/Jerry Tubby

(2.5 cm) of stem off. Alternatively, store the heads dry in a cool, draftproof place, with a maximum temperature of 40° F (4.5° C); they should keep for up to a week.

There is no special preparation needed, except for cutting off any remaining length of stem, very nearly flush with the base of the head for those to go at the top of the pyramid; others can have successively longer stems, depending on their position in the display. For transport to the show, pack them tightly between layers of tissue paper; it is not necessary to wrap each head individually. They look best when displayed simply in a shallow bowl or plate.

The judges will look for large, deep green, shapely heads, without any spininess or discoloration. The heads should be as uniform as possible and you should avoid showing one or two enormous heads which make the remaining ones look puny by comparison. Six perfectly matched moderate-sized heads are far more likely to be awarded high points.

Varieties

In the United States, only one variety is likely to be found widely:
Green Globe (Green Ball): compact growing but prolific variety; heads 5–7 in

(12.5–17.5 cm) across without prickles; available as seeds.

Other varieties
Vert de Laon: considered the best all-around variety in England. Heads flat, round, smooth and mild flavored.

Purple Globe: similar to Green Globe, but with purple tinge to flower heads.

Grande Beurre: produces consistently large and very fleshy heads; available as seeds abroad.

↟ *Vert de Laon, popular in England.*

↟ *Green Globe*

Pests & Diseases

Globe artichokes are for the most part trouble-free, and you are unlikely to meet with most of the problems mentioned below. Even then, you will find that none of the pests are serious, and are more likely to be inconvenient than damaging.

Petal blight: this is probably the nearest thing to a serious problem liable to affect globe artichokes. It is a fungal infection which attacks a wide range of plants, particularly chrysanthemums and dahlias in the flower garden. Cold, wet weather encourages the rapid spread of petal blight through the garden; otherwise, it tends to be localized.

On globe artichokes, tiny circular pale brown spots appear on the bracts and petals, and these enlarge and become darker brown. The discolored areas and even the whole bud may eventually rot. Because the spores of petal blight spend the winter in a dormant state on various weeds, the best precaution is to be sure that your garden is weed free, as far as possible. If the summer seems likely to be a cold wet one, spray the plants with an approved fungicide when the flower buds first start to form and repeat again seven to ten days later.

GUIDE TO ARTICHOKE TROUBLES

Symptoms	*Probable cause*
Light to dark brown, round blotches on bracts; blotches and whole bud may rot	Petal blight
Irregular holes eaten in lower leaves; slime trails nearby	Slugs
Plants fail to send up new growth in spring	Root rot

Remember that aphids and earwigs occasionally get between the bracts of the developing flower heads. There are no visible symptoms until the heads are in the kitchen, so always wash globe artichokes very thoroughly before cooking.

Step-by-step Growing Guide for Artichokes

➤Petal blight is a
fungal infection:
round, brown spots
are the main
symptoms.

Royal Horticultural Society, Wisley, Surrey

▼These artichoke
roots are infested
with aphids. A well-
cultivated, clean
garden is the best
preventive measure
against these pests.

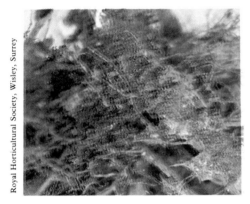
Royal Horticultural Society, Wisley, Surrey

Root rot: if globe artichokes are grown in waterlogged soil, then the roots become weakened and various soil-borne fungi may attack them. The first sign that something is amiss is in early to midspring, when new growth would normally be appearing. If you wait a few weeks and there is still no sign of new growth, then the plants are most likely dead, killed by root rot. The best precaution is to correct any drainage problems before planting the artichokes. Once they become infected, little can be done to correct matters and the plants should be dug up and destroyed.

Earwigs: these pests occasionally work their way into the developing flower heads, where they make ragged holes at the base of the bracts. Because the bracts fold over each other, this damage is not usually seen until the artichokes have been cut and are being prepared for the table. The best precaution is to be sure that the earwigs have no hiding places in your garden, such as piles of debris or weed infested hedgerows. Spray or dust the plants and surroundings, especially possible daytime hiding places, with Sevin if earwig infestation is particularly severe. Normally, all that is required is thorough cleaning of the heads before cooking.

Aphids: like earwigs, aphids occasionally find their way into the flower buds. Protected by the bud scales, they cannot be readily dealt with by sprays of insecticides. If your garden is well cultivated and weed free, and there are no other vegetables in your garden infested with aphids, then they should not be too troublesome. Again, clean the heads thoroughly before cooking.

Slugs: this pest rarely attacks the flower heads, which are carried well above ground level. Occasionally they will attack the lower leaves, nearer the soil. Ragged, irregular holes are the main symptoms, together with slime trails nearby. Slugs are particularly fond of the succulent blanched shoots grown under straw or compost, and the young leaves produced in spring. Control slugs with proprietary baits. Alternatively, trap them in piles of decaying vegetable matter placed at the base of the artichoke plants; inspect the traps daily and destroy any slugs found.

Asparagus

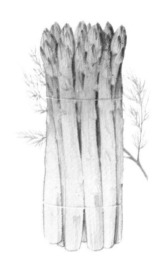

Asparagus officinalis (fam. *Liliaceae*)
Perennial with a useful life of at least 20 years
Size: grows in bush form to a height of about 5 ft (1.5 m)
Planting to harvesting time: from seed 3 years; from crown 2 years
Yield per plant (once established) is about 25 spears per year

Asparagus is a superb delicacy, and one which has always been relatively expensive to buy. As a crop, it is becoming increasingly popular with home growers with a reasonable-sized garden. The flavor of really fresh asparagus is unbeatable, and the initial effort of establishing a bed is an excellent long-term investment.

The young shoots, or spears, are the edible part of the plant, and are produced from early spring to early summer. The newly emerged shoots are light green with either green or purple tinged tips; they are whitish toward the base of the stem where the soil has kept the sunlight off. Although enormous shoots can be grown, and are good for exhibition work, asparagus are at their best, and also easiest to eat, when the stalks are 4–5 in (10–12.5 cm) long. If the stalks are not harvested, but left to grow on, the scales at the tip unfold and the plant produces tall, elegant stems with fernlike foliage.

The asparagus plant is a hardy perennial and very long-lived. Unfortunately, as a cultivated crop, asparagus has a somewhat bad reputation. The main deterrent is the three-year gap between sowing and the first harvest. However, the gap can be bridged by buying one- or two-year-old crowns from a nursery or garden center. In this way, cropping can begin in a relatively short time. Secondly, it is only a moderate cropper and

Marshall Cavendish/Donald Smith

◄*Although an asparagus bed needs time to become established, once it begins cropping it will crop for many years. This bed was planted over 100 years ago, and it still gives heavy annual harvests.*

GROWING ASPARAGUS FROM SEED

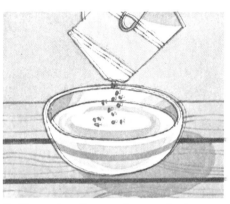

1. Select a sunny sheltered site; in spring, just before sowing, rake the soil to a fine tilth.

2. To make the seeds germinate more quickly, soak them in water for a few hours before sowing.

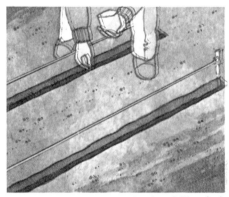

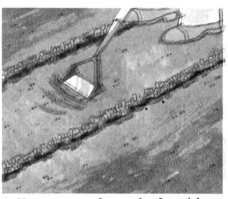

3. Sow the seeds thinly in drills 1 in (2.5 cm) deep, with 18 in (45 cm) space between the drills.

4. You can sow a few seeds of a quick germinating crop, such as radishes, with asparagus seeds to mark rows.

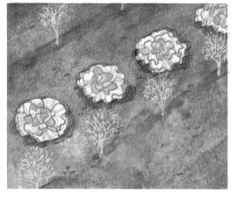

5. Thin seedlings first to 2 in (5 cm) apart, and then to 1 ft (30 cm) apart when they are 6 in (15 cm) high.

6. Sow catch crops, such as lettuce or carrots, between rows to make full use of the asparagus bed.

the season of cutting is short. However, a well established bed can continue cropping for up to fifty years, with the number and quality of the shoots improving annually.

It is not really worthwhile growing only one or two plants; for a family of four you should have at least twelve plants, with double or triple that number if you want a good steady supply. You need a lot of room for an asparagus bed, because the shoots sprout up over a wide area and cannot be contained in a small space. However, if you can provide the space, you will be amply rewarded with good crops of this delectable vegetable for many years to come.

Suitable site and soil
Asparagus will grow in a wide range of soils, provided there is proper drainage. Very heavy clays, acid peat, or thin soil over stone are not suitable. However, as long as the subsoil is free-draining, you can dig out the top 18 in (45 cm) of soil and replace it with more suitable soil. Although drainage must be first class, the soil should be reasonably moisture-retentive. Rich, sandy loam is best, and will give slightly earlier crops than those grown on heavy soils. If the soil is very heavy, it is best replaced; moderately heavy soils can be lightened with the addition of peat, compost, or coarse, gritty sand. Asparagus beds are normally on level ground, but if drainage is a problem, they can be raised about 2 ft (60 cm) above ground level.

A sunny site is best, and one that is open but not exposed to winds. However, asparagus will tolerate partial shade. Low-lying frost pockets are not suitable, as early crops could be damaged.

Growing from seed
Asparagus is relatively easy to grow from seed, and the initial cost is less expensive than buying crowns. However, there are several disadvantages as well. The main drawback is that it will take much longer to get crops from seed than from purchased crowns. Secondly, the seedlings will be very variable; many will be poor croppers and will have to be discarded. However, 1 oz (30 g) of seed will contain approximately 1,500 seeds; if you do not mind waiting the extra time, growing from seed is well worth trying.

Select a sunny, sheltered site for a seed bed, because the seedlings will remain there for two years before being planted into permanent beds. Prepare the bed well; it should be completely free of weeds, particularly perennials. As with permanent beds, the soil should be rich, with a good humus content—preferably well-rotted garden compost or farmyard manure. Autumn is the best time for preparation: the organic matter can then be well buried and the soil left rough during the winter.

Sow the seed in midspring; to hasten germination, it is a good idea to soak the seeds in water for a few hours prior to sowing. Sow them ½ in (1.3 cm) deep in drills 1 in (2.5 cm) deep, with 18 in (45 cm) between the drills. Sow the seed thinly, as germination rates are fairly high. The seeds should germinate in two to three weeks. You can sow a few seeds of a quick-germinating crop, such as radish, along with the asparagus seeds. The radishes will mark the rows so you can hoe between them without damaging the main crop.

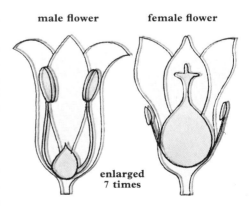

male flower   female flower

enlarged
7 times

Female asparagus plants are inferior croppers, and plants bearing female flowers should be removed.

Keep the bed well watered and free from weeds throughout the summer. Thin the seedlings to 2 in (5 cm) apart as soon as they are big enough to handle. Thin again to 1 ft (30 cm) apart when the plants are 6 in (15 cm) high. In autumn, when the feathery foliage begins to turn yellow, cut the plants down to almost ground level. Rake the bed and apply a mulch of garden compost or well-rotted manure. With new asparagus beds, you can make full use of the ground by sowing catch crops, such as lettuce or carrots, between rows. Once the beds are three years old, do not sow catch crops as they will compete with the asparagus for space, moisture and nutrition.

When the plants are mature, the females will produce berries. Female plants are inferior croppers; if you have enough male plants, root out the females and destroy them. You can also identify the sex of a plant by the flower formation because the male and female flowers are different (see diagram); plants bearing

female flowers should be removed. By this time the young plants should have a spacing of 1 ft (30 cm) and any extras should therefore be removed. If the plants are male, dig them up carefully and transplant to another site.

Preparing the permanent bed
Preparing the permanent bed for transplanting is the most important factor in growing asparagus successfully. This takes time and effort, but it is absolutely essential. The reputation of asparagus for being a difficult crop is almost entirely due to failures following inadequate preparation. Remember that asparagus has a very large and strong rooting system, and roots can go down 4 ft (1.2 m) into the soil, and spread sideways by that amount. This means that when you prepare the actual planting site, you should also prepare a strip 2½ ft (75 cm) wide on both sides of the bed, because the roots will extend sideways underground beyond the planting site. Asparagus beds are usually 4–6 ft (1.2–1.8 m) wide, so the total width of digging will be about 10 ft (3 m). It is a good idea to run a path on either side of the bed, so cultivating and harvesting can be carried out without treading on the beds and damaging the plants. Traditionally, asparagus was grown in trenches which were later earthed-up; today, they are more often grown on level ground. Whatever system you use, double dig the bed in the late winter, making the beds as long as is suitable for your garden. While you are digging, incorporate plenty of well-rotted manure, garden compost, similar material or seaweed if it is available, at the rate of one barrow load every 3 sq yd (3 sq m). You must get rid of all perennial weeds, or else your bed of asparagus will soon degenerate into little more than a weed patch.

This is also the time to correct any soil problems which would lead to failures in cropping if uncorrected. If the soil is fairly heavy, dig in old mortar, rubble, straw or sharp sand to improve drainage. If the soil is very light, work well-rotted

TRADITIONAL ASPARAGUS BED

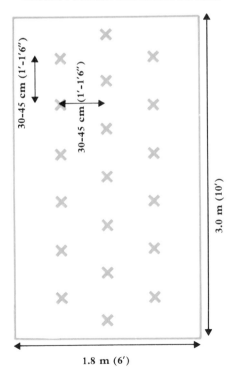

30–45 cm (1'–1'6")

30–45 cm (1'–1'6")

3.0 m (10')

1.8 m (6')

Step-by-step Growing Guide for Asparagus

PREPARATION OF PERMANENT BED

1. Dig in well-rotted garden compost or manure in the autumn, and leave the bed rough for the winter.

2. Remove all weeds from the bed, particularly perennial varieties, such as couch grass and thistles.

3. Just before planting, in early or mid-spring, dig out 1 ft (30 cm) deep trenches along the length of the bed.

4. Make a rounded ridge in the trench with fine soil; place crowns on ridge and spread roots out well.

5. Cover a few crowns at a time with soil so they do not dry out; continue until trench is completely filled.

6. After planting, firm the soil well; if the soil settles, top it up again with a little additional soil.

manure into the bottom spit. After preparing the beds, leave them rough, so that the soil is broken down by winter weather and made more friable.

If the soil is very stony, waterlogged or otherwise unsuitable, it is best to grow asparagus in raised beds. Construct retaining walls 2 ft (60 cm) high, 4–5 ft (1.2–1.5 m) apart, built with brick, stone, concrete or old railway ties. Fork over the soil at ground level to break up any hard pans and facilitate good drainage. Then dig in a layer of garden compost or well-rotted manure, and finish by forming a rounded mound of soil on top, about 1 ft (30 cm) high in the center.

Just before planting (in early or midspring, depending on weather), fork over the ground and rake it to a fine tilth. At the same time, if the soil is acid, apply a dressing of ground limestone to give it a neutral pH reaction, and fork it in lightly. Then dig out trenches 1 ft (30 cm) deep, along the whole length of the beds. A bed 4 ft (1.2 m) wide will take two parallel rows of plants; a bed 6 ft (1.8 m) wide will take three staggered rows.

When you have dug the trenches, form a ridge 9 in (23 cm) high with some of the excavated soil down the center line of each trench. The beds are now ready to receive the plants.

Setting out the transplants
Transplanting is best done in early or midspring, during dull weather if possible. If you have grown crowns from seed, you should be transplanting out two-year-old plants. If you are buying crowns from a nursery; make sure they are one or two years old, and no older. Although three-year-old crowns are occasionally offered for sale, they are much more difficult to transplant successfully, and are seldom as vigorous. One-year crowns are best.

For transplanting crowns grown from seed, only lift as many as you can plant in a short period of time; it is not necessary to lift all the plants at once. Quick planting is also necessary if you have bought crowns and they are delivered by mail. Although they travel well if properly packed, the crowns dry out very quickly once exposed to air.

▼*After cropping in spring, asparagus plants produce tall, attractive, fernlike foliage.*

Marshall Cavendish, Clay Perry

▲ *Harvesting of established beds begins in midspring, and continues for about a month.*

Allow 1–1½ ft (30–45 cm) between plants in the rows, and the same between rows. Asparagus roots are very long and should be spread out well over the ridge. Try to arrange the roots so that about half fall on each side of the central hump. Cover them with fine soil so that the tops of the crowns are 3–4 in (7.5–10 cm) below the surface of the soil. Then water thoroughly. Continue filling in the trench until it is level with the surrounding soil. The soil may settle a bit; if this happens, fill it up with more soil.

It is a good idea to keep a few plants in reserve, to replace any crowns which have not survived the transplant.

Care and development

While the young plants are developing, and before they can be harvested, they need careful cultivation. The beds always need to be kept well watered, particularly during hot, dry summers. Weeding must be carried out regularly during the growing season. Remember, though, that asparagus are also shallow rooted, and the roots are widespreading; avoid hoeing deeper than 2 in (5 cm) which would damage the rooting system. As the summer foliage grows taller it will need some form of support so it is not blown over. Use bamboo canes or stakes available from a garden center.

CARE

In autumn, when the foliage begins to turn yellow cut it down to ground level and burn it, tidy up the beds, and apply a mulch of well-rotted manure, seaweed or garden compost. This not only feeds the plants, but helps protect them from winter storms and severe frosts. In late winter, apply potash in the form of wood ash at the rate of 4 oz per sq yd (120 g per sq m). In early spring, apply soot at the same rate; this acts as a mild insecticide, releases nitrates into the soil, and, because it is dark, it helps retain soil warmth.

This same routine is carried out once the beds are established, with two additions.

Although it is not strictly necessary, some people apply agricultural salt (common rock salt) to established beds, because asparagus in its natural state is usually found near the sea. Apply it at the rate of 2 oz per sq yd (60 g per sq m), in midspring, and twice again at monthly intervals. As well as supplying the asparagus with nutrients, this helps to destroy seedlings of annual weeds.

In autumn you can ridge up the established plants after mulching. Dig a shallow layer of soil from the space between the rows of plants and pile it over the crowns. The ridges are forked over lightly in early spring and leveled out in midsummer. Ridging up is not strictly necessary, however, and good crops of asparagus can be grown entirely on the flat.

Forcing

If you want out-of-season asparagus, from late winter onward, there are several methods of forcing. Crops can be grown in a heated greenhouse, on hotbeds, or in their permanent beds by using a portable cold frame. It is best to use four-year-old crowns for lifting and forcing, and ones which you have not cut from previously. Unfortunately, crowns which have been lifted from their permanent beds and forced will be completely worn out by the end of the season, and should be discarded.

1. Although not strictly necessary, you can apply rock salt in midspring to established beds.

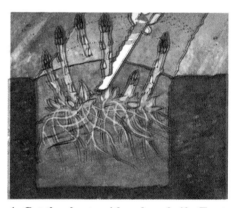

4. Cut the shoots with a sharp knife. Try to cut as close to the base of the stalk as possible.

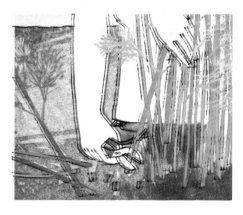

7. Cut foliage down to ground level in autumn, when it begins to turn yellow, and tidy up the beds.

Step-by-step Growing Guide for Asparagus

AND CULTIVATION

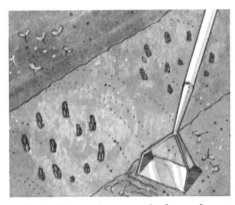

2. Hoe lightly to keep weeds down; do not hoe deeply or you may damage the shallow roots.

3. The first year you harvest, pick only two or three stalks from each plant, early in the season.

5. After harvesting, keep the beds well-watered, particularly in long spells of hot, dry weather.

6. Use bamboo canes or stakes to support summer foliage so it is not blown over by wind.

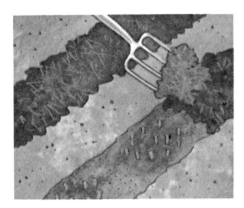

8. After cutting down foliage, apply a mulch of well-rotted manure, seaweed or garden compost.

9. In late winter apply potash to the bed in the form of wood ash, and rake it in very lightly to avoid damage.

FORCING ASPARAGUS

1. Place a cold frame on top of the bed in midwinter; fill the frame with a 4 in (10 cm) layer of garden compost.

2. Close the frame lid and cover with sacking; surround the frame with fresh manure as insulation.

To force asparagus in heated greenhouses or in hotbeds, lift the crowns in late autumn, after the foliage has died down; make sure you leave plenty of soil around the roots. Store the crowns in a cold dark place for about a week, and keep them moist. For greenhouse forcing, plant the crowns close together under the shelves in boxes 9 in (23 cm) deep, covering them with 4 in (10 cm) of finely sifted soil. Maintain an air temperature of 62.6° F (17° C) and a steady supply of moisture; they should be ready for cutting three weeks later.

For hotbed forcing, a similar air temperature is also needed. Make the bed out of three parts leaves and one part stable manure by bulk. Cover the hotbed with a frame. When the temperature of the mixture, measured by using a soil thermometer, reaches 62.6° F (17° C) put a 3 in (7.5 cm) layer of potting mixture over the bed; place the crowns on top and spread the roots out. Just cover the crowns with a further layer of sifted soil mix and water well. About two weeks later, cover with an additional 6 in (15 cm) of fine soil. Cropping should begin about three weeks later, and continue for a month. After cropping is finished, throw the crowns away. Plants can be forced in succession, so that spears are available between midwinter and early spring.

For forcing asparagus outside in permanent beds, place a cold frame on top of the bed in midwinter, and fill the frame with a 4 in (10 cm) layer of leaf litter or garden compost. Then close the frame, and place mats on the glass as further insulation. Finally, surround the frame with fresh manure, well consolidated, up to 1 in (2.5 cm) below the top of the frame. This method of forcing can supply asparagus from late winter until midspring. Toward the end of cropping, leave a few sticks on each crown, so the plant can recover. It will probably take a couple of years for the plants to recover completely and crop well. You should not try to force the same crowns in successive years; each year move the frame to a different area of the bed.

Harvesting
Although it may be very tempting, do not cut any shoots for the first two seasons after planting. This allows the plants to become settled and build up strength for future cropping. During the first cutting season, take only three shoots from each plant. Do this at the beginning of the season, which may be late midspring or late spring, depending on locality, leaving later shoots untouched.

Once the bed is firmly established, inspect the plants two or three times a week. Cut every shoot that appears, from late midspring onward. Some of the shoots, of course, will be straggly and thin. Pick these and use them in soups. If you leave them on the plant, they will use up resources that should go to more vigorous shoots.

Harvesting of established beds should stop after six weeks; the remaining shoots will manufacture food and strengthen the crown for the following season. Although the delicate foliage is very attractive, do not cut it to use for floral arrangements, otherwise the plant will be weakened.

The actual process of cutting the shoots may seem difficult at first, but it becomes easier if you keep in mind the

↟ *Ready for cutting.*

↟ *Bundled for storage.*

way asparagus grows. Underneath the surface of the soil, the crown is producing many small shoots, at various stages of maturity. If you are not very careful when cutting the shoots you wish to harvest, you may cut these off as well, and the plant will stop cropping. Try to confine cutting to as close to the base of the stalk as possible. Cut the shoots when they are about 3–4 in (7.5–10 cm) above the surface of the bed. Carefully scrape the soil away and cut the shoot obliquely, about 3–4 in (7.5–10 cm) below the surface. You can use a sharp kitchen knife, or a special asparagus knife, obtainable from your nurseryman or garden center.

Cut shoots soon lose their freshness; ideally you should cut them an hour before cooking. If you want to keep the cut stalks longer, stand them with the cut end in a dish of water, and place the dish in a cool place, or wrap them in plastic and store in a refrigerator. You can also freeze asparagus successfully for a welcome winter treat.

Exhibition tips

Because asparagus is very sensitive to changes in temperature, it is best not to cut shoots too hard for a week or so before the show. This way, even if there is a sudden cold spell, you will still have a reasonable choice of shoots when the time comes to cut them.

Cut the shoots with a sharp knife, about 3 in (7.5 cm) below ground level. The length of the stem is determined by the thickness. Although the optimum length is 9 in (23 cm), with 4 in (10 cm) of green stem and 5 in (12.5 cm) of blanched stem, very thick shoots can be up to 12 in (30 cm) long. Thin shoots, on the other hand, would be best shown at a slightly shorter length than 9 in (23 cm). After cutting, tie the shoots into temporary bundles, and store them upright in a cold, dark place so the scales do not open. Thirty-six is the usual number specified. If no number is given, use as many shoots as needed to give a pleasing exhibition. For very thick stalks, 25 should be enough; for slender stalks, a bundle of 50 would make a better display.

Just before the show, cut the bases square, and make all the stalks the same length, so that when they are displayed in a bundle, all the tips are level. If there is any soil left on the stalks, clean them with a damp sponge; do not scrub them or you will bruise the skin. Asparagus are usually shown in bundles, tied with two strings. Stand the bundle up in a basket 2 in (5 cm) deep and slightly wider than the diameter of the bundle. Pack the basket with moss, and decorate the surface with parsley sprigs. The judges will look for straight, brightly colored, plump stems with the scales closed; short, crooked, thin or shriveled stalks, or those with the scales open, will be considered defective.

If the bundles have to be packed for transport to the show, wrap each bundle in paper and lay them in boxes, one bundle to a box. At the show, remove the bundles immediately, or the heads of the stems will try to grow upright, and form right-angled bends.

Varieties

Brock's Imperial: an F hybrid, very early; vigorous and prolific. Good in South; moderately rust-resistant.

Mary Washington: the leading commercial variety for years; rust-proof, early, productive. Good for freezing and canning.

Paradise: highly rust-resistant; large, crisp, tender and mild. Very early.

Roberts: a new improved strain of Mary Washington; large, tender, very prolific.

Viking: another improved Mary Washington; popular in Canada.

Viking 2K: also Canadian; selected for disease-resistance and vigor.

Waltham Mary Washington: another improved strain for northern conditions.

Pests & Diseases

Asparagus beetle: this is a fairly common pest. It is usually less damaging than the asparagus fly, although occasionally severe infestations occur. The beetles have reddish wing cases, with black crosses; they are sometimes called "cross-bearer beetles" for this reason. The grubs are gray and humpbacked; unfortunately, several generations are produced each summer. First the shoots, and later the ferny foliage are attacked. Infested shoots look one-sided, and are much more vulnerable to secondary infections. Foliage which has been attacked shows dark, withered patches. Besides reducing the existing crop, if the plant is seriously weakened, its future cropping ability can be lessened. A good precautionary measure is to clean the beds thoroughly in autumn and burn all the debris. If your plants are attacked, spray with derris or pyrethrum as soon as the pests are seen, which is usually from early summer onward. You will have to spray several times for the derris or pyrethrum to be completely effective; nicotine may also be applied, but do not use this spray during the cropping season if you want to harvest stalks.

Asparagus rust: this fungal disease is usually worse during humid, hot weather in late summer; the main symptom is the appearance of rust colored spots on the shoots. Good preventive measures are dusting the top growth with flowers of sulfur at monthly intervals, cutting off and burning any infected shots, and cleaning the beds properly in autumn.

Asparagus fly: this tiny insect appears in mid or late spring, and lays its eggs in the asparagus stalk. The emerging tiny, white, legless grubs tunnel into the stalks, usually several to a stem. Young infested shoots become distorted and stunted; the foliage of older plants will turn yellow prematurely, and the stalks may break off at ground level. As with asparagus beetle, cleaning the beds and burning all debris is an effective precau-

GUIDE TO ASPARAGUS TROUBLES

Symptoms	Probable cause
Shoots one-sided, foliage dark, withered	Asparagus beetle
Shoots distorted and stunted, foliage turns yellow prematurely	Asparagus fly
Irregular holes in the shoots, silvery slime trails nearby	Slugs
Rust colored spots on shoots	Asparagus rust
Foliage yellow, roots enmeshed in violet strands	Violet root rot
Blackened, withered tips	Frost damage

Royal Horticultural Society

▲ *The asparagus beetle larva attacks shoots and foliage; may seriously damage crops.*

Ministry of Agriculture, Fisheries and Food

▲ *Violet root rot, a soil-borne fungal disease, cannot be cured; destroy all infected plants.*

tion. When cutting down the stems in the autumn, make sure you cut them as low down as possible, so that no pupae are left to hibernate in the stems. Cut off and burn any suspect stems. If the infestation is severe, grub out and burn all plants, and do not replant the site with asparagus for several years.

Slugs: these common garden pests find young asparagus shoots very attractive. Symptoms of slug attack are irregular holes in the shoots and silvery slime trails nearby. Slugs can be picked off by hand or caught in traps made of vegetable refuse, such as orange peels. If you use traps, inspect them daily and destroy any slugs found. If slug damage is severe, use slug pellets containing metaldehyde.

Violet root rot: this is a serious fungal disease which attacks other vegetables besides asparagus. Parsnips, carrots, beets and potatoes are also vulnerable to infection. It is a soil-borne disease, and roots of infected plants when lifted show webs of violet strands enmeshing them. The aboveground symptom of infection is yellowing of foliage. There is no chemical cure for root rot; grub up and destroy infected plants. Do not replant the site with asparagus, or other susceptible vegetables, for several years.

Frost damage: although not really a disease, late frosts can damage new growth. Frosted tips will be blackened and withered; unless severely damaged, the plant will send up new growth.

Broad Beans

Vicia faba (fam. *Leguminosae*)
Hardy annual
Sowing to harvesting time: 9–12 weeks
for spring sowings; longer for autumn sowings, depending
on the climate
Size: standard varieties 2–4 ft (60–120 cm)
Yield: 11 lb (5 kg) per 10 ft (3m) double row

Once an extremely common vegetable, the broad bean is now less widely grown. Nevertheless, the ancient broad bean is an undemanding and rewarding early summer vegetable and is eminently suitable for the amateur gardener. It is the first legume to produce a crop in the early summer, and fresh young broad beans are a welcome change from the winter greens which are the most readily available alternative at that time of the year.

The broad bean is a distinctive plant with a square, erect stem, which can be up to 3 ft (90 cm) tall in most varieties, and is occasionally branched. It is pollinated by insects and bears clusters of white, black-blotched flowers in the axils of the leaves. The fertilized flowers develop into pods which hang down from the leaf axils and, depending on the length of these pods and the number of beans in them, broad beans can be divided into two types. Longpod varieties have the longer pods containing about 8 rather oblong beans; Windsor varieties have shorter pods containing fewer large, circular beans. Longpods are extremely hardy and in most areas can be

sown in the late autumn to produce an early crop. Windsor varieties are later, producing a heavy crop of flavorsome beans in summer from a spring sowing.

If you buy broad beans from a store they are invariably too old and have become hard and unappetizing. Home-grown broad beans, however, can be picked when they are still young and tender—a totally different proposition.

Choosing a site
Broad beans do best on an open site but they are not fussy and will grow quite happily anywhere in most gardens. You should select your site rather with the interest of other crops in mind. When fully grown the bean will form a hedge up to 4 ft (120 cm) tall which will shade any rows of plants to the south of it. You should make sure that plants on either side get sunshine during at least part of the day by planting the beans so that the rows run north/south. It makes sense, too, to plant the beans alongside a crop, such as lettuce, that will appreciate the shelter the beans provide in early summer; spinach is another crop which benefits from shade in hot weather.

Preparing the soil

The best soil for broad beans is a rich heavy loam, well-manured from previous years and deep enough for the plants not to become short of water in the summer. Although broad beans are leguminous plants which obtain nitrogen from the bacteria in their root nodules (and leave the ground richer than they found it) they appreciate additional nitrogen in their early stages. Organic matter also helps by keeping the ground moist during the summer. If the beans can follow on land well-manured from a previous crop, this is ideal.

Do not worry, however, if your conditions are not perfect. Broad beans will do well on most soils provided that they are not waterlogged. If the beans are to follow another crop directly, just dig the soil well before sowing. If not, the land should be prepared in the autumn. Dig the soil deeply, adding garden compost or well-rotted manure if the soil lacks it—a good general rate is about 10 lb per sq yd (4.5 kg per sq m). For spring sowings leave the ground rough so that it can be better broken up by the frost and add a further light dressing of compost two weeks before sowing.

▼ *Broad beans are an excellent early summer vegetable.*

Marshall Cavendish/Clay Perry

SOIL PREPARATION AND SOWING

1. Two weeks before sowing add superphosphate at a rate of 2 oz per sq yd (60 g per sq m) and rake in.

2. Use a draw hoe to take out a wide shallow drill 2½ in (6.3 cm) deep and 4 in (10 cm) wide.

3. Sow the seeds in a double row with the seeds in one row opposite the gaps in the other.

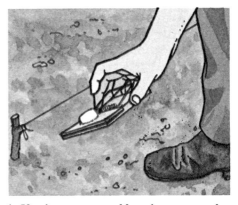

4. If mice are a problem in your garden place traps at intervals along the row and inspect the traps often.

Broad beans dislike an acid soil so test your soil and, if acid, add lime as indicated by a soil test kit.

A few days before sowing, add superphosphate, at the rate of 2 oz per sq yd (60 g per sq m). Rake in carefully, so as to produce a level seedbed.

Sowing

Broad beans have the biggest seeds of any of the common vegetables, so they can be planted individually just where they are destined to grow. The best method is to prepare shallow drills 2½ in (6.3 cm) deep and 6 in (15 cm) wide.

Then place the beans in a double row with one row down each side of the drill. Leave 10 in (25 cm) between each bean in a row. Place the beans in one row opposite the gaps in the other row. If you are planting more than one double row, leave a space of 2½ ft (75 cm) between each so they do not overshadow one another.

The germination rate of broad beans is low—less than 75 percent—so sow a few extra plants at the end of the row and transplant them to fill in gaps. Alternatively, if space is limited in a small garden, you can sow two double rows just 4–6 in (10–15 cm) apart. As germination is rarely 100%, overcrowding is unlikely to occur. The result of planting like this is a hedge of beans 1–1½ ft (30–45 cm) wide.

Broad bean seeds will germinate at any temperature above freezing and the bright green seed leaves should emerge above ground 1-2 weeks after sowing.

Spring-sown beans

The commonest time to sow beans outdoors is from late winter to early spring depending on local weather conditions. You can plant in the late winter if you have a sheltered garden with a mild climate but should wait until the middle of early spring in colder and more exposed places. The beans from these sowings will be ready for picking from the beginning of early summer. If you want an earlier crop you can start the seeds in a cold frame up to a month sooner.

Broad beans are a cold weather crop and do not do really well during the heat of the summer. Nevertheless, staggered sowings will give you crops throughout the summer in many areas. You can sow in midspring to pick in late summer and again in early summer for an early autumn crop.

Autumn-sown beans

The hardy broad bean can withstand severe frosts as low as minus 15°–20° F (−9.4° to −6.6° C) and is thus suitable for autumn sowing in all but the coldest areas.

There is often little advantage in autumn sowing, however, unless you plan to use the broad beans as wind protection for another crop. Autumn-sown broad beans may crop only 2–3 weeks earlier than spring-sown beans and are also less likely to be attacked by bean aphids, but against these advantages there is always the possibility that a cold, wet winter will destroy the crop entirely.

Some gardeners protect autumn-sown beans with plastic tunnels but, even if these are available, risks are involved. If the winter is mild the beans will grow so strongly that they will have to be uncovered in the early spring. A sudden severe cold spell, once the protectors have been removed, could then kill off all the early growth.

Dwarf beans

If you do have such protection available for broad beans you are better advised to grow a dwarf variety if you can find one. These plants grow to about 1–1½ ft (30–45 cm) tall, so they are unlikely to become too big too early in the season. They are also useful in a small garden where there is not room to grow taller varieties. Do not expect such a heavy crop as you would get with taller varieties, however.

Sow a dwarf variety in single rows with 10–12 in (25–30 cm) between plants and 1–2 ft (30–60 cm) between the rows, depending on the variety. The plants will grow to produce a bush with three to five stems about 1½ ft (45 cm) wide.

Care and cultivation

Regular hoeing around the plants is necessary, especially when they are small. Additionally some weeds grow up within the rows very close to the beans. Do not risk trying to remove these with a hoe. Pull them up by hand.

In a wettish year, broad beans will not need watering, as the early summer soil should still be fairly moist. They cannot withstand drought, however. If the soil does begin to dry out, as it may well do for late crops, water generously.

Although they are not true climbers broad beans are nevertheless tallish plants with a good deal of bushy foliage, which is supported by quite shallow root systems, so you will need to give all but dwarf varieties some help against the wind to prevent them being blown down. Small plants can be supported by earthing up for about 3–6 in (7.5–15 cm) around the stems (this also gives some protection against very cold or very wet weather for beans sown in late autumn, and over-wintered) and by placing twigs in the ground alongside the plants in the same way that you would for peas.

CARE AND CULTIVATION

1. Draw soil up around the bases of young plants to give them support and to protect them from the weather.

2. Hoe carefully to remove weeds. Pull up by hand, any weeds growing very close to the plants.

3. Broad beans may be blown over in windy weather. Support them with stakes and string.

4. Pick off the growing points. This is done to deter bean aphids and to encourage bigger pods.

Twigs are not sufficient, however, in windy areas, particularly on sandy soils. In such areas, tie the plants in with string. Place thin stakes or canes at 3 ft (90 cm) intervals down both sides of the double rows close to the beans. Then tie around the stakes with twine 1 ft (30 cm) and 2 ft (60 cm) above the ground. The beans can then lean against this pen in windy weather. As the plants grow, re-move the sideshoots from the base of the stems while they are still small, so that each plant has only one main stem. As soon as each plant has set about four or five flowers, pinch out the growing points at the top of the stems. This has two uses. It encourages the formation of pods and also discourages aphids which like to feed on the growing point and youngest leaves.

CARE AND CULTIVATION

5. Immediately after removing the tops spray with rotenone or pyrethrum to control bean aphids.

6. Harvest the beans with a quick downward twist of the hand. The lower pods mature first.

If the growing points are clean they can be either cooked and eaten like spinach or added to your compost heap. If they are infested with aphids, however, burn them to destroy the pests.

As broad beans are leguminous plants, obtaining nitrogen indirectly from the soil atmosphere through their root nodules, they do not need any feeding once they are growing.

Harvesting
Harvesting broad beans is a matter of taste. If you like mature, hard beans, then leave the pods on the plant until they are beginning to become bronze in color, before picking. Most people, however, prefer more tender beans. For these, the pods should be picked as soon as sizeable beans can be felt inside. It is a good idea to open one pod, which will indicate if others of the same size are ready. The beans should be a good size but still soft. Alternatively, for a really tender vegetable, try picking very young pods and cooking them, pods and all, as you would for snap beans.

When you pick your beans, do it by a quick downward movement of the hand.

Aftercare
After the main crop has finished, broad beans often send up suckers which, if left, flower and eventually produce beans. A second crop can be obtained in this way—especially if the old growth is cut out to encourage the suckers. The number of beans which can be collected is normally very small, however, so unless space is no problem in your garden (in which case you may as well have this little extra crop), cut off the plants at ground level once the first beans are harvested and use the land for something else. Still leave the roots in the soil, though, as the nodules on them contain nitrogenous salts which will help the next crop. Brassicas would be a good follow-up as they are a leafy crop needing quite a lot of nitrogen.

If the ground is required immediately for another crop, add the discarded top growth of the bean plants to your compost heap. If not, dig the entire plants,

BEANS

GROWING UNDER GLASS

1. Sow the seeds individually in 4 in (10 cm) pots in late winter or early spring. Sow a few more than you actually need.

2. After sowing place the pots out in a cold frame or put them on the shelves in a greenhouse.

3. The seedlings are ready for planting out in early or midspring. Take care not to damage the root ball.

leaves, roots and stems, well into the soil (chop them up if necessary) and let them rot. They make an excellent green manure.

Growing under glass
Broad beans can be sown in pots, in an unheated or a heated greenhouse, or in a cold frame, and then planted out in early spring for an early crop. Use one pot for each seed so that the root is disturbed as little as possible when transplanting. Remember that the germination rate is only 75 percent, so allow for this by sowing a few more seeds than you actually need.

Raising in pots and then planting out is often the only way of getting early broad beans in areas where winters are too severe for autumn planting and the ground is unsuitable. to work before midspring.

Exhibition tips
To get really good broad beans for showing, they should be grown on a rich, heavy soil. Beans grown on a sandy soil are rarely as good. It is very difficult to give broad beans too much manure or garden compost, so add as much as you have to spare during the autumn digging.

You must sacrifice some of the total crop if you wish to grow broad beans for show, since the best beans are produced when only one pod is grown on each cluster. Remove all the pods competing with the one destined for show as soon as the pods have formed. It also helps to grow as many plants as possible, so as to increase your choice when making the final selection.

Select fresh, green, young and well-filled pods without blemishes. They should be large but of a uniform size. The beans inside should be young and tender. Old beans show a black mark on the side, which indicates the point at which the bean germinates; this is considered a blemish.

Broad beans wilt very easily and keeping the beans fresh for showing is a problem. Leave picking as late as possible and then store the pods in a damp cloth to reduce transpiration. Sometimes an ugly heel is left on the pod after picking and this should be removed with a sharp knife.

The common number of pods exhibited is 18. Simply place them neatly together across a plate or on the table.

Varieties

Aquadulce Claudia: hardy, medium flavored, early long pod; sow in fall or very early spring.
Broad Windsor Long Pod: one of only two widely available in the United States; upright, best early spring planted.
Dreadnaught: long pod type, well flavored, good quality.

Express: Fast-maturing, sow early spring. Short-podded; top quality, heavy producer.
Fava: the other variety widely sold in the United States; short-podded. Does not like heat, can be fall-planted.
Frostproof: plant as soon as ground is workable; dwarf, short-podded.
Imperial Green Long Pod: green-seeded, heavy cropper; sow in spring. Excellent exhibition sort; flavor medium.
Kodrin: dwarf with up-facing pods; plant 25 percent closer than all others for heavy crop.
Masterpiece: very tasty, green-seeded; medium pods. Very adaptable to conditions.
Teizeroma: large pods of good quality; bears over long period.

▲ *Aquadulce Claudia*

▲ *Imperial Green Long Pod*

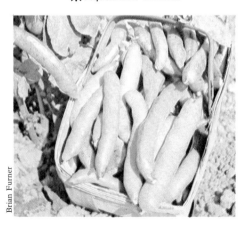

▲ *Frostproof*

▲ *Broad Windsor Long Pod*

Other varieties

Bunyard's Exhibition Long Pod: white-seeded; hardy early croppers; well-filled pods about 12–16 in (30–40 cm) long.

Imperial White Long Pod: white-seeded; long broad pods with up to 9 beans; excellent for exhibition.

Masterpiece Green Long Pod: green-seeded; long pods; excellent for exhibition, very good flavor.

Red Epicure: brown-red seeds which become straw-colored when cooked.

Imperial White Windsor: white-seeded; heavy cropper; up to 8 beans per pod.

Giant Four-seeded Green Windsor: green-seeded; heavy cropper; short pods with 4 or 5 beans per pod.

Imperial Green Windsor: green-seeded; up to 7 beans per pod.

The Sutton: white-seeded dwarf type; plants about 1 ft (30 cm) high; pods about 5–6 in (13–15 cm) long; 5 seeds per pod but dwarf beans will give smaller crops than the normal-sized varieties.

Pests & Diseases

By far the most troublesome pest of broad beans is the aphid. Happily, however, it is quite easily controlled. If your broad beans escape the aphid, few other pests or diseases are likely to be a serious problem. But it is well to be on the lookout also for the pea and bean weevil, a beetle that eats leaf edges in a somewhat scalloped pattern.

Bean aphid: these tiny insects suck the sap from the plants and foul the leaf surface with a sticky black substance called honeydew. The earliest crops are usually unaffected as they produce beans before the aphids have become established, but later crops may be heavily infested.

The aphids congregate particularly on the growing point but are also found on the stem and on the undersides of leaves, which may curl up if badly attacked. Taking out the growing points of the beans reduces the likelihood of attack, but is unlikely to protect the plants completely. Spray or dust the plants with rotenone or pyrethrum as necessary.

There is some evidence that summer savory discourages aphids. Try sowing some between the rows of beans.

Chocolate spot: brown spots and streaks on the leaves, stems, petioles, and sometimes also the pods, of the plants are a sure sign of an attack of chocolate spot caused by forms of the fungus botrytis. Good healthy plants, growing on fertile and well-drained soils are never seriously attacked, although autumn-sown plants which have been weakened by frost are susceptible. However, even these plants are likely to recover without treatment. The disease is only serious if the soil lacks either lime or potash and

Harry Smith Collection

▲ *Express*

Brian Furner

▲ *Fava*

the season is wet. The best defense is to plant only in good, well-manured soil, and to space the plants adequately.

Bean beetle (Bruchid beetle): these beetles are not a serious threat to a growing crop but damage seed which is being stored for future planting. The adults look similar to weevils, lay eggs on the pods of growing plants or on seeds in storage; the legless and curved grubs bore into the seed, feed and pupate inside it. Because of the size of the bean seed, germination is not usually affected but the holes made in the seed reduce the amount of food available to the germinating seedlings, resulting in stunted plants in severe cases. They also expose the seeds to attack by other borers such as millipedes and wireworms, which may be in the soil at sowing time, and to fungal and bacterial diseases.

Seeds containing live grubs or beetles should be burned. They should not be placed on a compost heap, as the beetles may spread from it. As the pest is seed-borne the surest precaution against it is to buy seed only from a reputable merchant.

Pea and bean weevil: the same weevil which attacks peas also attacks broad beans. The weevils eat semicircular holes from the edges of young leaves and also eat the nodules on the roots. Dust or spray the plants with rotenone.

Mice: occasionally seed can be correctly sown in good land, and few or no seedlings germinate. This is probably the result of attacks by mice which take the seed and store it. Set traps at intervals along the rows, and inspect the traps frequently.

Royal Horticultural Society, Wisley, Surry

▲ Aphid: the worst pest of broad beans.

A. A. Turner

▲ Bean weevils eat holes in the leaves.

GUIDE TO BROAD BEAN TROUBLES

Symptoms	Probable cause
Small black insects on stems, leaves and growing points; curled-up leaves	Bean aphid
Chocolate-colored spots on leaves	Chocolate spot
Seed leaves misshapen, seedlings stunted, small holes in seed	Bean beetle
Semicircular holes along leaf edges	Pea and bean weevil
Complete failure to germinate	Mice

Pole Beans

Phaseolus coccineus (fam. *Leguminosae*)
Perennial cultivated as **half hardy annual**
Sowing to harvesting time: 8–10 weeks
Size: This depends largely on the variety used, but normally they are picked when 6–12 in (15–30 cm) long. Plants 6–10 ft (1.8–3 m) high
Yield: 1½–2 lb (0.75–1 kg) per plant, or 10 lb (5 kg) per yard (meter) of row

Reliable and easy to grow, the pole bean is often known as the "amateur's vegetable." Its ornamental flowers and succulent green pods have made it a firm favorite. Pole beans are perennial plants in their South American homeland, but in cool temperate areas they are grown as annuals from seed to avoid their susceptibility to frost.

As part of a good rotation plan, pole beans should follow brassicas (cabbage family) or potatoes. Like other members of the family *Leguminosae,* pole beans possess root bacteria which convert nitrogen gas from the air to nitrogen compounds, thus enriching the soil for a following crop.

Selecting a site
Pole beans do best in a site that is both open and sheltered. Windswept sites and low-lying frost pockets are not suitable, because in windy or cold weather pollinating insects do not visit the flowers. Avoid planting your beans near any gaps in fences or hedges through which frost might enter.

When deciding where to plant your pole beans, remember they grow very densely, and a row of climbing beans will make a solid wall of foliage 6 ft (2 m) high. This will shade adjacent rows of vegetables on either side for several hours a day, even if the bean rows run from north to south. Site them accordingly, perhaps at the end of a plot, or next to a wall.

Preparing the soil
The ideal soil for pole beans is a rich, loamy one, well supplied with moisture. Provided that the upper layers are well drained, the more moisture the better; good bean crops are dependent on adequate water. Avoid heavy clay soil as it is generally much too cold at sowing time; very shallow or sandy soils are not suitable as they tend to dry out in summer.

Well before planting time, dig your bean trench. This should be 1 ft (30 cm) deep and a minimum of 2 ft (60 cm) wide. On soil with a high clay content, deeper digging to a depth of 1½ ft (45 cm) will help improve drainage.

CULTIVATION

1. Prepare trench well before sowing; double dig and incorporate manure.

2. Two weeks before sowing, apply superphosphate and potash.

3. Rake in the fertilizers, and level off the bed.

4. Sow in drills under protective covers for early sowings, or in cold areas.

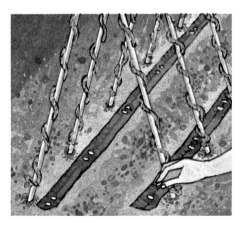

5. Position canes and twine; sow in deep drills, two seeds per cane.

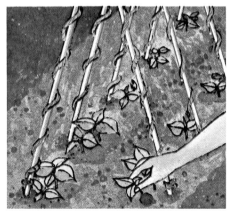

6. As seedlings start to grow, cut or pull out the weaker of the two.

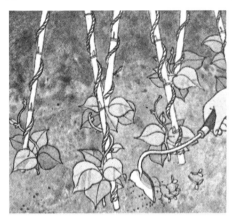

7. Weed around young plants taking care not to damage them.

8. As plants wind themselves up the framework, tie in any stray growth.

9. When plants have reached the top of supports, pinch out growing point to encourage lateral growth.

10. When watering, soak the ground completely to reach the deeper roots. A light sprinkling is simply harmful.

11. Mulch over wet soil in early summer, to preserve soil moisture.

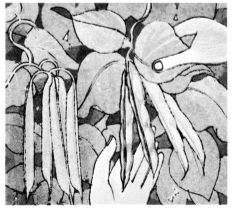

12. Keep picking regularly. Discard yellow, gouty pods—they are too old.

It is very important to dig organic matter into the bottom spit, or spade depth, of the trench to help keep the soil open, friable, and moist; it will also serve as a source of nourishment for the growing plants. Well rotted manure or garden compost, at the rate of a 2-gal (10 L) bucketful per sq yd (sq m) is sufficient; dig it in during the fall or early spring to allow time for the soil to settle before spring sowing.

When preparing the soil, one point to remember is that too much nitrogen in the soil is sometimes a cause of bean flowers failing to be successfully fertilized, or "set." This is best prevented by avoiding fresh manure or artificial fertilizers known to have a high nitrogen content. As a precaution, 1½ oz (45 g) of superphosphate and ½ oz (15 g) of sulfate of potash per sq yd (sq m) applied to the ground immediately prior to planting will balance the presence of too much nitrogen.

Soil in industrial areas or towns is often prone to acidity; beans crop poorly on soil which is too acid. The ideal pH for this vegetable is between 6.0 and 7.0. Test your soil; if it is less than 6.0 add ground limestone at the rates suggested in the soil test kit.

Sowing

Allow five or six plants per person; if you wish to freeze surplus crop allow double that amount.

Pole bean seeds are usually sown outdoors in late spring to provide a crop from midsummer to midautumn. In especially warm and sheltered areas, however, it is possible to sow outdoors during midspring to give a crop starting in early summer. Because the plants are tender and susceptible to frost, and because the seeds will not germinate unless the soil has warmed up, protection is needed for earlier sowings. This initial protection is particularly necessary if you live in a cold district.

The shelter for the young plants can be plastic tents, or a greenhouse or cold frame in which the seedlings can be raised in boxes. They can then be hard-ened off and planted out after all danger of frost has passed. Pole beans can also be raised in pots; peat pots are useful because you won't disturb the roots at planting out time. If you decide to use peat pots, remember to thoroughly wet the pots at planting out time; otherwise the dry pot will impede the flow of moisture from the soil to the plant's root system.

The rate of germination of pole beans is usually very high (80 percent or more). But it is still wise to sow a few extra seeds at one end of the row, so you will have a few replacement seedlings if there are failures in the row caused by poor germination or by pest damage to the germinating seedlings.

For planting, draw out a 2 in (5 cm) deep drill, water it, and sow two seeds every 12 in (30 cm) in either one or two lines depending on the method of support. If you are growing the beans up a single row of poles, sow one line only. If you are going to support the plants with pairs of crossed beanpoles, sow the seeds opposite each other in a double row 1 ft (30 cm) apart. If you are going to use netting, sow two rows, again 1 ft (30 cm) apart, with the seeds staggered. If you are planting more than one double row of pole beans, they should be at least 5 ft (1.5 m) apart.

As soon as germination has taken place, earth-up around the plants to protect them from possible frost damage. If they do suffer frost damage, pull them out. If it is not too late, make a replacement sowing, because frost-damaged pole beans will never fully recover. Stake the young plants as soon as possible to protect them from wind.

Methods of support

Whatever method of support you use, it must be absolutely rigid. One heavy cropping plant can weigh up to 4 lb (2 kg) and a whole row of them will be enormously heavy. A 10 ft (3 m) row of beans 6½ ft (2 m) high will have a surface area of about 7 sq yd (6 sq m) of dense foliage. This is extremely vulnerable to strong wind; once a row of beans

TRAINING METHODS

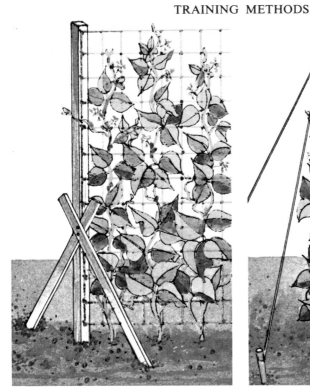

On netting: fix net to posts placed 6 ft (1.8 m) apart, sunk 18 in (45 cm) in ground.

Rows of canes linked by wires, with stout poles and guy ropes either end.

has collapsed it cannot be re-erected. It will smother neighboring rows of vegetables, and must be removed at once.

The simplest method of support is to give each plant one cane, or pole, pushing it 1½ ft (45 cm) into the ground, with 6½ ft (2 m) above ground. If you have access to a wooded area, you can cut your own bean poles; alternatively, 8 ft (2.4 m) long bamboo canes, with a 1½ in (3.8 cm) diameter at the thick end, may be used. Each cane is then linked to the next by thin wire or strong twine. At both ends of the row, two much stouter poles are inserted. Lateral stability is provided by straining wires from these heavy end poles to pegs driven into the ground, in the same way as guy ropes are used when putting up a tent. If the row is very long, you may need intermediary posts and struts halfway along the row. Permanent clothes posts or nearby trees can be used to secure the end posts.

Another common method of support is to use the bean poles in pairs; they are inserted into the ground at an angle, so that the tops cross each other at a height of about 5½ ft (1.6 m). The poles are tied together at the crossing. After a row of these pairs of poles has been erected, 1 ft (30 cm) apart, more poles are laid horizontally in the crotches formed, overlapping, and securely tied to the intersecting vertical poles where they meet. These horizontal poles help keep the framework rigid. If you are using bamboo canes, it is a good idea to twine string up the length of the smooth canes, to give the climbing bean vines something to cling to.

A third method is to grow the beans up netting, supported between strong posts. Use 4 in (10 cm) mesh wire, plastic coated wire or plastic netting. Posts supporting the netting should be 8 ft (2.4 m) long, hammered 1½ ft (45 cm) into the

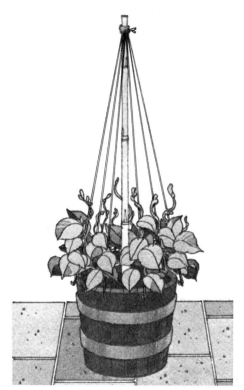

Growing in a tub: use a central pole and twine hooked to edge of tub.

Wigwam of bamboo poles, tied at the top, twine twisted around poles.

ground at each end of the row, and at 6 ft (1.8 m) intervals along the row. Two internal struts are required for each post, to take the weight; these struts reach 3 ft (90 cm) up each pole and are well buried in the ground (see diagram).

If you are only growing a very small number of beans, wigwams of 6 or 7 poles planted in a circle and tied together at the top will suffice. The plants may be a bit crowded at the top, but will otherwise grow well. Pole beans can also be grown in a large tub, with strings tied to the top of a central pole, and radiating out to hooks which have been fixed to the tub (see diagram). A tripod with three canes is an alternate method of supporting beans grown in a tub.

When the first vines start to search for something to climb, tie them loosely with raffia or string to their own poles. This is very important; once the beans have begun twining round each other for lack

of proper training it will be impossible to disentangle them. Most people give each plant a pole, stick or string; some growers, however, allow up to four plants to use the same support. Choose the method you prefer.

Once the beans have started climbing up the supports, there is no training necessary until the tips reach the tops of the supports. Then pinch off the growing points. This encourages the production of lateral shoots further down the plant, and helps to increase crop yield.

Care and development
The main requirements of the growing pole bean plants are simple enough: moisture, weeding and feeding. The crop will not be successful if the plants are allowed to get at all dry. During spells of dry weather, water the plants at least twice a week. You must use enough water to soak the ground completely and

➤*Bush or dwarf
varieties, when
available, do not
need support and
are ideal for grow-
ing under protec-
tive covers.*

Eric Crichton

reach down to the lowest roots. Light sprinklings can actually be harmful, as they encourage the deep-feeding roots to come to the surface, where they are vulnerable to hot sun and drying winds. If you are growing your beans in tubs, water them daily during droughts, as soil in tubs or pots dries out very quickly.

In dry conditions, mulching is helpful, as it slows the rate at which water evaporates from the soil. Lawn mowings, 2 in (5 cm) deep, are often used as a bean mulch; bark fiber, if you can obtain it, is a particularly good mulch because water and liquid feeds can penetrate to the soil below. Apply mulch in early summer, making sure the soil to be mulched is moist.

Liquid feeding can be occasionally in-corporated into the watering pattern as soon as the plants are flowering. Make a dilute liquid feeding by soaking a bag of manure in a tank of water until the fluid is the color of weak tea, or use a soluble chemical plant food.

While the seedlings are developing, you must weed regularly. Hoe the weeds while they are still small, taking care not to harm the delicate roots and stems of the young beans. Once the beans are growing well, they cast a heavy shade which keeps down most weeds; hand weed as necessary. Mulching the plants also helps smother any weeds which might develop.

Failure of the flowers to set is sometimes due to hot, dry weather conditions. Spraying the beans with a fine misty spray every morning and evening, under and over the foliage—in addition to regular waterings—may help. Plants grown on moisture-retaining soil should not suffer too badly in a drought.

Bush plants

Some gardeners train climbing pole beans as bush plants This is done by pinching out the growing points at the first joint as soon as the young plants begin to climb. When the plants are 1 ft (30 cm) high, nip off the growing tips of the lateral runners to promote bushy growth. You must continue removing these tips at weekly intervals for the plants to remain compact.

Harvesting the crop

Pole beans will be ready for picking in mid to late summer, and the golden rule is to keep picking. You must look over plants every few days during the harvesting season, and pick off all young tender pods. Length is not a reliable guide to ripeness, as the length at which they are ready to be picked depends on the variety. In general, beans which have grown too long have coarse-textured, pale pods, and the beans inside are hard and tough. These are inedible and should be discarded. Be careful to remove all old, stringy beans which have been overlooked under the dense, leafy growth; as long as these remain on the

To train as bushes, pinch out growing point, then growing tips of laterals.

plant, further bean production is reduced.

Remember to remove slug-damaged, badly twisted or muddy pods as well, as they reduce the cropping potential of the plant and may invite infection. Pick the beans early in the morning or evening if the weather is hot. If you don't use them right away, store them in a cool place, where they will keep for a couple of days, or in a refrigerator, where they will keep a bit longer. The best solution is to either freeze the surplus beans, if the variety is suitable, or share them with friends or neighbors.

At the end of the season, when clearing the plants after final harvest, leave their roots in the ground. They are rich in nitrogen and will improve the soil for a following crop.

Exhibition tips

If you want to grow beans for exhibition purposes, you will be losing some of the total crop weight the plant would have otherwise produced, as you must remove all pods competing with the few grown for exhibition.

Treat the plants normally until you have pinched them out two leaves above the last flower truss when they have reached the top of the bean poles. Then stop all laterals two leaves above a flower truss. Three weeks before the show date, begin feeding your plants regularly with liquid manure. About a fortnight before the show, select the most promising of the pods, marking them with a bit of string. Then thin the trusses to two or three pods, supporting the weight of the beans by tying them in lightly to the poles or netting. Remember to remove the other beans from the plant, so they don't absorb nourishment intended for the show pods.

The length of the beans exhibited depends on the variety, but they can be 15–20 in (37.5–50 cm) long and 1 in (2.5 cm) wide. Besides length, the judges will consider the beans' color and texture. A top quality pod will be young, fresh and crisp, without any bumpiness from swelling seeds.

Clay Perry M.C.

◀A row of well-trained pole beans makes an impressive and attractive garden feature.

An exhibition dish of pole beans usually contains 24 pods, as alike as possible. If some beans reach their prime condition a few days before the show, cut them off, leaving 1 in (2.5 cm) of stalk on the pods. Store them stalk downward, until the show, in a jam jar containing ½ in (1.3 cm) of water which is changed daily.

On the day of the exhibition, choose your best pods and lay them neatly and as straight as possible on a large plate or across the bench.

Some exhibitors save home-grown seed from year to year. This is a dangerous practice, because of the high risk of seed-carried infections and insects.

Storage

During processing of beans for freezing or canning, handle them carefully to prevent damage. Store in containers with smooth inner surfaces. Crushed, cut or decaying beans should be picked out to avoid disease or decay among the healthy vegetables.

To dry beans for storage, leave pods on the vine to mature. When they turn a beige color, remove the beans from the pods and place for an hour in a 130–145° F (53–63° C) oven to kill any bean weevils.

Varieties

Pole beans are the most valuable bean type for the home gardener and may be grown in all parts of the United States and Canada. The plants produce green, yellow and occasionally purple pods.

Blue Lake (White Creaseback): straight, unusually smooth, stringless; a favorite for freezing, canning. Vigorous, prolific; pods round, meaty, moderate length.

Burpee Golden: pods wide, flat, butter yellow; tender, fiberless, meaty. Starts like bush, then climbs.

Crusader: red-flowered; pods long, straight, to 20 in (50 cm), yet crisp and tender. Prolific.

Desiree: new, vigorous even in dry seasons. Very productive; pods stringless, fleshy, tasty.

McCaslan: pods moderately long, round, fleshy, good quality; also doubles as shell bean.

Missouri Wonder: produces large crops even under trying conditions; pods long, round, tender. Good for planting among corn.

Purple Podded: climbs well, prolific; large, meaty, stringless. Red-purple pods turn green in cooking.

Romano (Italian Pole): long, wide pods with distinctive flavor. Stringless, tender, meaty; good freezer.

Scarlet Emperor: a good, heavy cropper with smooth pods. Good for eating, exhibiting.

Scarlet Runner: an old favorite grown primarily for color; pods good for table when young.

Kentucky Wonder: the old standby; foolproof and productive. Rust resistant;

Brian Furner

▲ *Scarlet Emperor*

Brian Furner

⋏ *Sunset, a British variety.*

⋏ *Enorma, popular abroad.*

Brian Furner

Pat Brindley

⋏ *Achievement, exhibited in England.*

⋏ *Goliath, also known as Prizetaker.*

Harry Smith

Brian Furner

⋏ *Crusader, heavy cropper.*

⋏ *Streamline, good tasting.*

Brian Furner

pods stringless, good quality. Also good as shell bean.

Kentucky Wonder Wax: moderately long, brittle, meaty; use as snap beans when young, shell beans later.

Scotia (Striped Creaseback): good cornfield sort; pods light green, purple-spotted, almost stringless.

Other varieties
Zebra: attractive mottled long pods; heavy cropper with aromatic flavor, suitable for freezing.

Fry: white seeded, white flowers; long pods; good cropper during hot, dry weather; suitable for freezing.

Streamline: pods very long; scarlet seeded; not suitable for freezing; good flavor.

White Achievement: white seeded, white flowered general purpose pole bean; kitchen or exhibition quality; pods very long; not suitable for freezing.

Enorma: heavy cropper; pod very long; suitable for freezing.

Sunset: pale pink flowers, heavy cropper, can be grown up supports or as bush beans; not suitable for freezing.

Brian Furner

▲ *Desiree*

Pests & Diseases

Pests and diseases can destroy much of the hard work put into a home garden— if you let them. So make sure your garden plan includes a knowledge of those that may attack the vegetables you intend to grow and how to control them. Doing so is much easier with today's fungicides and insecticides, and it is well to remember that nonchemical preventive measures are very effective, too. These include choosing disease-resistant plant varieties, using seeds from a reliable source that have been treated with a fungicide, planting in different areas of the garden, and destroying any infected plants. Remember, never place diseased plants on the compost heap.

Some insects—aphids, for instance— can be washed off beans and other plants with a stream of water from a hose. Others, such as the Mexican bean beetle, hibernate through the winter and lay their eggs in weeds and other garden debris. So by cleaning up your garden in the fall you will discourage that type of pest from settling in, ready to feast on your next year's crop. Lastly, the use of paper collars over seedlings helps protect them from ground-level attacks by cutworms and certain beetles.

If it does become necessary for you to use a fungicide or insecticide, be sure to follow the label directions carefully, paying special attention to the specified time for stopping applications before harvesting. Of course, chemicals or not, always wash garden vegetables thoroughly before using them.

Pole beans are relatively trouble-free, but may be affected by any of the following:

Mexican bean beetle: the chief pest of beans, once a local pest in the Southwest, it is now troublesome over much of the United States with one to four generations per year, according to climate. Black-spotted yellow adults winter over in rubbish and weeds, appearing in late March in the South, in June in New York. After feeding on the leaves a week

▲ *Damaged and distorted pole bean leaves: the effects of various beetles.*

▲ *An infestation of black bean aphid on a pole bean shoot.*

or two, yellow eggs are laid on the undersides of the leaves. Upon hatching, soft yellow prickled larvae skeletonize the leaves from below. To control, clean up all rubbish and weeds in the fall and spray plants with Sevin or rotenone as soon as the insects appear, repeating as necessary.

Other beetles: to a lesser degree, beans are also attacked by various cucumber and flea beetles as well as sundry other pests such as the Fuller rose beetle of the South Atlantic states and California. However, all are controlled with the sprays mentioned above.

Bean beetle (maggot): eggs of this beetle are laid on the growing seed pod, or on seeds which have been dried and stored. After hatching, the legless and curved grubs enter the seed and bite a round hole beneath the surface skin of the seed. The damage done by these pests is twofold: because the growing grub feeds on the seed, the amount of nourishment for the seedling is diminished, if the germinating seedling is not killed outright. Secondly, the holes made by the beetles allow such other pests as millipedes and wireworms to enter, and expose the seed to attacks by fungal and bacterial growths. Any seeds found to contain living grubs or beetles should be burned; they should *never* be placed on the compost heap or left lying about. Because these pests are seed carried, you must be

absolutely certain that your seeds are from a reliable source. The bean weevil does much the same type of tunneling, but is most troublesome in beans stored for eating. Heat to 135° F (57° C) for three hours.

Slugs: one of the most familiar of all creatures which attack plants, they feed chiefly after dark, both above and below ground. They will attack the leaves, stems, roots and pods. During the day they hide away in dark, moist, cool places and decaying vegetable matter. To control, scatter slug bait around the plants in the evening. Repeat if necessary.

Cutworms: like slugs they hide by day, eating through seedling stems (close to the ground) by night. Also controlled by the slug baits.

Bean aphid: this is a black aphid which completely smothers the growing points of beans in late spring. The affected plants stop growing, and the few pods which develop are covered with a black, sticky substance. It can be controlled by spraying with Sevin or rotenone, repeated as necessary. The infected tops of plants can be removed as soon as enough pods are formed.

Bean anthracnose: this disease is sometimes called "blight," "rust" or "canker," and thrives in damp, wet conditions. The

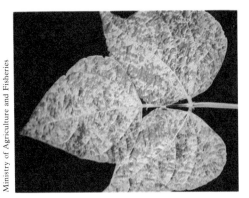

Ministry of Agriculture and Fisheries

Murphy Chemical Co.

▲ Signs of viral infection: yellowish areas spreading through the dark green of the leaf.

▲ Later stages of "blight": the transparent ringed spots dry up and leaf begins to wither.

symptoms are black spots which soon grow into sunken, circular pits surrounded by red lines. Leaves, stems, and pods may be affected. The disease penetrates the pods and infects the seeds, which then develop brownish-black markings. Mildew and rust also attack beans in moist weather. All three are controlled by spraying with a state-recommended fungicide, and it is better not to work among the plants when they are wet.

Root rot: this occurs most often on soils which are cold and badly drained; the roots are weakened and made liable to attack from soil fungi. When this happens, dark brown or black spots can be seen on the roots and stems, just below the soil level. As with all seed-borne diseases, the best precaution is to obtain seed from a reliable source.

Nematodes: these almost microscopic "eel worms" burrow into the roots and greatly weaken the plants, even though all the growing conditions seem favorable. Short of sterilizing the soil, the best control is to plant marigolds among the beans.

Birds: in some areas these can also be troublesome, pulling the seedlings out of the ground. Check them by placing tunnels of fine wire fencing over the rows of young plants.

GUIDE TO POLE BEAN TROUBLES

Symptom	Probable cause
Leaves eaten by black-spotted yellow beetles, or skeletonized from below by yellow larvae	Mexican bean beetle
Leaves and/or stems eaten	Various other beetles
Irregular holes in leaves, stems and pods; faint silvery trails	Slugs
Seedlings eaten through near ground	Cutworms
Sunken black spots, edged in red, on leaves, stems and pods	Bean anthracnose
Plants covered with small, black, sucking insects	Bean aphid
Plants weak, show poor growth in spite of everything else favorable	Nematodes

Snap Beans

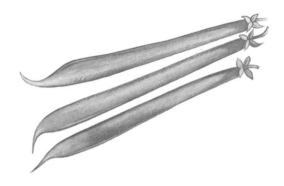

Phaseolus vulgaris (fam. *Leguminosae*) also known as French bean and string bean
Half-hardy annual
Sowing to harvesting time: 6–8 weeks
Size: dwarf varieties 6–12 in (15–30 cm) high, 6–12 in (15–30 cm) across; climbing varieties up to 8 ft (2.4 m) high
Yield: 20 lb (9 kg) per 30 ft (9 m) row for dwarf varieties; 30 lb (13.5 kg) for climbing varieties; 2 lb (1 kg) as dried haricots

Snap beans make an ideal crop for the home grower; the plants are compact, require little attention, and the yield of succulent, delicately flavored pods is high compared to the small amount of space needed. Except for protecting early and late sowings from frost damage, little is needed in the way of cultivation, and the plants for the most part take care of themselves. Once they are growing well, the large, attractive leaves form a dense canopy which acts as a weed suppressor. The thick foliage completely shades the soil beneath, and weeds, starved of sunlight, are unable to compete. Snap beans will crop well in spite of long periods of drought, although heavier crops will result if they are watered regularly in dry conditions. As an additional bonus, the leaves, white or lilac-tinted flowers, and pods, colored purple or scarlet in some varieties, are exceedingly decorative, and a few plants will enhance any border.

There are both dwarf and climbing varieties available. The dwarf, or "bush," type grows 6–12 in (15–30 cm) high, while the climbing varieties can be up to 8 ft (2.4 m) tall; these have growing habits similar to pole beans and will need some form of support. The pods of both dwarf and climbing varieties are 3–6 in (7.5–15 cm) long and hang beneath the leaves.

Although most varieties have green pods, some are mottled red and white. Snap beans with pale yellow pods are called "waxpod," or wax beans, and are thought by many to have the finest flavor of all. The pods are round or flat in section.

Because these beans are only half-hardy in cool temperate climates, they are normally cropped outdoors from midsummer through to midautumn. By successional sowing, and by giving some protection, you can extend the cropping period by a good two months, from early summer past the early light frosts.

The beans can be harvested at various stages of development. When the pods are very young and delicate, they are

Pat Brindley

▲ *Succulent snap beans ready for harvesting; outdoors, cropping begins in midsummer.*

picked for cooking whole. When slightly larger and more mature, the pods are harvested and cut up into pieces before cooking. If left on the plant to grow, the beans inside the pod will begin to swell. These beans are then shelled, and served when green, or allowed to grow to full maturity, and then dried for winter use. As a general rule, the more snap beans you pick, the heavier the crops will be, as frequent picking encourages the development of more pods.

Suitable site and soil

Snap beans do best in a sunny, sheltered situation. They will grow in almost any soil, but prefer one that is not too heavy.

A heavy soil can be lightened by working in peat, garden compost or coarse sand.

Ideally, you should grow snap beans on a plot well manured for a previous crop, such as spinach. If you have no such site available, dig in manure in the autumn before planting, at the rate of one bucketful per sq yd (sq m). The soil pH should be as near 7.0 (neutral) as convenient. Test your soil some months before planting, and correct if necessary with the addition of lime.

This crop does especially well if potassium and phosphorus are given as base dressings, so a couple of weeks before sowing or planting out, dress with sulfate

SOWING AND EARLY CARE

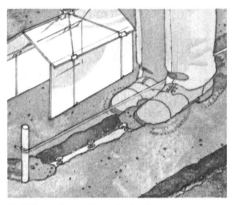

1. **When the soil and air temperature are warm enough, sow seeds in pairs, 6–9 in (15–23 cm) apart in seed drills.**

2. **To keep pods from dragging on the ground, support plants with pea sticks or short lengths of bamboo.**

3. **While the plants are young, hoe to keep weed competition down, and also to keep soil surface broken up.**

of potash, at the rate of ½ oz per sq yd (15 g per sq m) and superphosphate at 1 oz per sq yd (30 g per sq m) and fork in well.

Sowing
Theoretically, snap beans can be sown outdoors from mid or late spring, with successional sowings every two weeks right through late summer, for late autumn cropping. However, germination will not take place unless there is a minimum temperature of 60° F (15.5° C), and bean seeds planted in cold wet soil will quickly rot.

Because the plants are subtropical in origin, they cannot tolerate frost, so early and late sowings will need protection if they are to be at all successful. Local weather conditions are a major factor, and the last frost date varies from year to year and from place to place. A basic understanding of the plants' temperature requirements will help you to avoid disappointment, and you can select the right sowing time for your particular garden.

Generally, for early summer crops, sow in midspring. Main crops can be sown outdoors from then on. Beans grown for drying should not be sown later than the beginning of summer, as they need plenty of time for proper ripening.

The seeds vary enormously in size, shape and color, according to the variety selected, but even the smallest are easy to handle and can be sown individually. Because the success rate of germination is relatively low (75 percent), it is sometimes helpful to sow the seeds in pairs; if both germinate, cut the top off the weaker seedling when the first true leaves appear.

The distance between seeds and rows of seeds varies according to the time of year planted, the planting position, and harvesting requirements. Whatever the planting spacings, make sure the soil has been worked to a very fine tilth. If there are stones or rough lumps of soil, the emerging seedlings will be stunted or misshapen. Drills for snap beans should be 2 in (5 cm) deep. If you are growing the beans against a wall or fence, then only one row of plants is needed. Otherwise, sow the seeds in double rows, 1 ft (30 cm) apart. If you have more than one double row, leave 2–3 ft (60–90 cm) between them, so that you can cultivate and pick the crops easily. However, if you are planting beans for drying, the rows need only 1 ft (30 cm) between them. This is because the shell beans are usually harvested all at once, so easy access to every plant is unnecessary.

Sow the seeds at 6 in (15 cm) intervals for early crops and shell beans, and 9 in (23 cm) intervals for main crops. Germination should take place between 10 days and three weeks after sowing. It is not necessary to water the beans while they are germinating but soaking before sowing helps germination. A word of advice: never leave unused beans on the surface of the soil, or birds will immediately be attracted to the site and quickly peck up the beans. If you have been troubled by birds in past years, it is a good idea to protect the seeds and seedlings with wire mesh netting, similar to that used for peas.

Transplanting
Snap beans grow best when sown directly where they are to grow. However, for very early crops, and in cold districts, you can sow pairs of seeds in boxes or pots in the greenhouse, four to six weeks before the last expected frost date. Because snap beans do not transplant well, and tend to stop growing once disturbed, it is best to sow them in peat pots which can be planted out without any disturbance to the roots. Another method is to sow the seeds in blocks of turf, which can then be planted out in late spring.

Care and cultivation
Snap beans will produce heavier crops when regularly hoed and watered. Watering is particularly important in dry weather, when the crop's growth is liable to be checked, and the flowers may not set. If the flowers wilt and droop, the insects cannot penetrate and pollination will not take place. When this happens, spray the plants with a fine misty spray every morning and evening until the flowers have set. This fine mist will not be sufficient to keep the soil moist; a thorough watering, directed at the plants' roots, will also be necessary in dry weather.

Regular hoeing not only keeps weeds under control, it also keeps the surface of the soil broken up. In prolonged dry spells, some soils, particularly if watered by hose, form a hard surface crust. This prevents water penetrating the soil, and it runs off the surface without reaching the plants' roots. Hoeing also creates a dust mulch, which helps conserve soil moisture. A mulch of clean straw or leaf litter has the same effect, provided the soil is thoroughly watered before the mulch is applied.

Small doses of liquid manure are beneficial. To make, soak a bag of manure in a tank of water until the liquid is the color of weak tea.

Strictly speaking, the dwarf varieties do not need support. However, they tend to get weighed down by the pods, which then rest on the ground and become vulnerable to slug attacks. In wet weather, they will get covered with mud, too. As a precaution, support the plants by tying them to short lengths of bamboo. Occasionally, dwarf varieties will send out runners in an attempt to climb; cut these off as soon as you see them.

The climbing varieties need the support of tall rods or canes around which they will twine in the same way as pole beans. Erect one rod or cane per plant; these should be about 6 ft (1.8 m) high after they have been pushed well into the ground. The framework will consist of a line of pairs of canes, straddling the axis of the row, not less than 18 in (45 cm) apart at ground level. Alternatively, use string or large mesh netting for support. Earthing-up around the base of the plant, up to the first set of leaves, gives additional support to the stem, as well as encouraging extra root growth.

CARE AND HARVESTING

1. If it is hot and dry when flowering occurs, spray plants daily with a fine mist of water to aid pollination.

2. A mulch of clean straw, moist peat or leaf litter conserves soil moisture and helps keep down weeds.

3. When harvesting, cut the pods with scissors or pull the pods off with care or you may damage the plant.

If you made late sowings and plan to harvest right through autumn, give the plants protection as needed if frost threatens.

Greenhouse growing

If you have a heated greenhouse with an air temperature of 60° F (15.5° C) and a minimum soil temperature of 55° F (12.7° C), you can grow good crops of out-of-season snap beans in the ground. Greenhouses which are glazed down to ground level are best, as the snap beans need plenty of sunlight. You can also grow them in frames, but only if you live in a really warm and sunny area.

Sow the seeds in a good quality seed mixture, with enough heat, any time from late summer to late winter. Expect cropping from late autumn through to early spring. For minimum root disturbance during transplanting, use peat pots or sow the seeds directly onto soil blocks. Once the first pair of true leaves are showing, transplant them into the ground beds. The soil should not be too rich, or the plants will make excessively leafy growth at the expense of pod formation. Ideally, soil which has been manured from a previous crop is best.

Space the plants 9 in (23 cm) apart, in single rows 12–15 in (30–37.5 cm) apart in frames and in double rows about 1 ft (30 cm) apart in the greenhouse. Climbing varieties grown in the greenhouse will need support. Use strong garden twine, fixed vertically to two parallel, horizontal wires. The top wire can run under the roof, and the lower one should be about 6 in (15 cm) from the ground. Two plants will climb up the same string.

Cultivation is the same as for outside growing, but make sure the plants are kept growing in a reasonably moist atmosphere, otherwise red spider mite could become a major problem, and ensure that the glass is as clean as possible, to allow maximum light to reach the plants.

Harvesting

The beans are ready for picking from six to eight weeks after sowing, depending

◄*Planting distances between snap bean plants depends on when and where they are sown, and whether they are to be harvested over several weeks, or picked all at once, for drying and storing.*
Usually, they are planted in double rows, 1 ft (30 cm) apart, leaving 2–3 ft (60–90 cm) between each set of double rows. This allows for easy access to cultivate and harvest. Rows of shell beans are usually planted much closer together, as they are harvested all at once. Remember that climbing beans can overshadow lower-growing vegetables, so site them carefully.

Marshall Cavendish/Clay Perry

on weather conditions. Once the pods have started to form, check them daily, as they mature quickly. Most varieties are best when about 4 in (10 cm) long. Unless you are growing the crop specifically for the seeds, do not allow the ripe pods to remain on the plant. If you do, the seeds will grow larger, but the texture and flavor of the pod itself will deteriorate. Secondly, the plant will concentrate its energy on the swelling seeds, at the expense of pod production, and your crop will diminish accordingly. Daily picking will ensure that cropping continues for several weeks.

When tested, pods ready for eating will snap cleanly in half, without any stringy fibers. The beans inside will be visible, but will not have expanded to their full size. Cut or pull the pods carefully from the plant. You can sever them with thumb and fingernails; the plants are very shallow-rooted and you may pull the whole plant out of the ground if you pull too hard. Snap beans are best eaten on the day of picking, because, although they are excellent for deep freezing, they do not otherwise store well. If you plan to shell the half-ripe beans, leave the pods on the plants until they are just beginning to look more mature. At this stage, the beans should be pale green. They can either be cooked fresh or dried for later use.

Shell beans

The beans of some varieties, if left to ripen fully, can be dried and stored for winter use. In midautumn, when the pods are pale brown and beginning to split, the beans are ready for harvesting. Cut the plants down, shell the pods, and spread the brown or white beans out on clean paper or wooden trays to dry. The floor of a greenhouse is a suitable drying place, but any room which is light and airy will do.

Some autumns turn cold and rainy before the pods have fully ripened. If this happens, dig up the plants, and hang them upside down in a shed or attic. The pods can then finish ripening under cover; once the pods are brittle, shell and dry the beans in the usual way. When the beans are dry, store them in glass jars with tight-fitting lids.

Aftercare

When cropping is over, cut off any remaining growth above ground level. If it is healthy and free from insects, place it on the compost heap. Otherwise, burn all stems and foliage to minimize the spread of pests and diseases. As with all leguminous crops, these bean roots will increase the nitrogen content of the soil as they decay. This is particularly important if the following crops grown on the site are nitrogen-hungry, such as brassicas and potatoes.

Exhibition tips

There is no special cultivation required for growing exhibition snap beans; if you follow normal cultivation procedures and your plants are growing well, you should have plenty of pods up to show standard. One useful hint: these beans, when quickly grown, sometimes look a bit pale. To prevent this, give a light dressing of nitrate of soda, at the rate of 2 oz per sq yd (60 g per sq m), when the young plants start forming true leaves.

➤*Snap beans are excellent subjects for growing in pots, either in the greenhouse, or out-of-doors, in a warm, sunny spot. Remember that soil in pots dries out very quickly, so water frequently in warm weather. Otherwise, cultivation is the same as for snap beans that are grown outdoors.*

Brian Furner

Step-by-step Growing Guide for Snap Beans

HARVESTING AND DRYING SHELL BEANS

1. **Harvest for shelling in midautumn, when pods are pale brown and beginning to split; if it is cold and wet, pull up plants and hang indoors to ripen fully.**

2. **Spread shelled beans on trays, and dry them in a well ventilated room.**

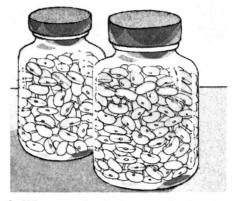

3. **When completely dry, store in glass jars with tight-fitting lids.**

Midspring sowings outdoors should give ripe beans for early to midsummer shows, provided the weather has been reasonable. If you live in a particularly cold district, it is safer to sow in peat pots in a cold frame in spring, and plant out at the beginning of early summer. For late summer or autumn shows, cover possible crop failures by sowing small successional batches, say, at two week intervals, until midsummer.

The judges will look for straight, fresh, tender pods without any bumpiness; keep this in mind when selecting the beans. Twenty four beans are usually required, but it is safer to pick about twice this number, so you will have plenty of reserves at the show bench. Completely ignore enormous pods, which are likely to be tough and fibrous; they will not gain you any points.

To keep your beans from looking tired and stale, pick them at the last possible moment before the show. Make sure your hands are clean, because it is difficult to wash stains off the pods without destroying the bloom.

As soon as the pods have been collected, lay them out on damp, clean cloths, and then roll the cloths up into loose bundles. They can travel to the show like this, provided they will not remain in the bundles for more than two days. If there is a longer interval between picking and the show date, it is best to pack the beans dry. A couple of hours before displaying, immerse the pods in cold water to restore their crispness.

BEANS

Beans look nicest when displayed in a circular pattern on a plate, if permitted. The tails of the pods should face outward, toward the edge of the dish.

Pests & Diseases

The kitchen garden can be destroyed by pests and diseases. Your garden plan should include learning about pests and diseases that may attack the crops you intend to grow and how to control them. Though there are many fungicides and insecticides on the market, it is well to remember that preventive measures are effective too. Choose disease-resistant plant varieties, only use seed that has been purchased from a reliable source, rotate your crops and destroy all infected plants.

Some insects can be washed off plants with a stream of water from a hose. Other insects hibernate through the winter and lay their eggs in weeds and other debris. If you clean your garden in the fall, you will discourage that type of pest from settling in. The use of paper collars over seedlings helps protect them from attack by cutworms. If you use chemicals, be sure to follow the label directions.

Bean beetle (Bruchid beetle): because this pest resembles a weevil, it is sometimes called, incorrectly, "bean weevil." The female lays her eggs on the growing seed pod, or else on seeds which have been dried and stored. Once the legless grubs hatch out, they bore into the seeds, and then bite a round, windowlike hole beneath the skin surface; it is through this hole that the adult beetle eventually emerges.

Besides feeding on the seed, the holes that they make allow secondary infections, such as fungal and bacterial diseases, to enter. Remove and burn any seeds or pods which are holed, or contain living grubs. Because these pests are usually seed-carried, the best precaution is to be sure your seeds are from a reliable source.

Slugs and cutworms: these familiar garden pests feed on a wide variety of plants. Active chiefly after dark, they attack leaves, stems, and pods, biting large holes in them. During the day, they hide away in dark, moist, cool places. Slugs are often found in decaying vegetable matter, and on soils which are rich in humus and moisture. Closely allied with slugs are cutworms which attack by chewing through the stem close to ground level.

One method of destroying them is to trap them. Place wet sacks, or heaps of damp vegetable refuse, such as cabbage or lettuce leaves or orange peels, at the base of the bean plants. Inspect the traps daily and destroy any captured pests.

Alternatively, control with prepared baits.

Bean aphid: this insect is most troublesome in late spring, when it attacks the growing points of beans. Plants infested with bean aphids stop growing, and the few pods which develop may be covered with a black, sticky substance. Control by spraying with pyrethrum or rotenone, and repeat as necessary. Remove and burn infected tops of plants as soon as enough pods have formed.

Mexican bean beetle: once a local pest in the Southwest, it is now the chief pest of beans over much of the United States with up to four generations per year, depending upon the climate. Black-spotted yellow adults hibernate in weeds and rubbish and appear in late March in the South; in June in New York. After feeding on the foliage a week or two, yellow eggs are laid on its underside. Upon hatching, the soft yellow prickled larvae skeletonize the leaves from below. To control, clean up all rubbish and weeds in the fall and spray the beans with Sevin or rotenone as soon as the pests appear, repeating as necessary.

Other beetles: to a lesser extent, other beetles also attack beans. Some are the Fuller rose beetle of California and the South Atlantic states, Japanese beetles,

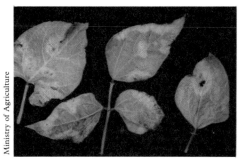

▲ *These leaves show the main symptom of halo blight: spots surrounded by yellow rings.*

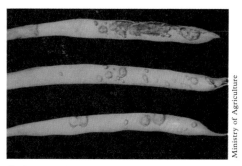

▲ *Round, dark, sunken spots on bean pods are telltale signs of anthracnose infection.*

the various cucumber beetles and flea beetles. To control, spray with Sevin or rotenone.

Nematodes: these almost microscopic eelworms burrow into the roots and greatly weaken the plants, even when all other factors seem favorable. Short of sterilizing the soil, plant marigolds among the beans as the most effective control.

Red spider mite: this minute sucking insect pest occasionally attacks snap beans, especially if grown in hot, dry conditions. Watch for the appearance of leaves heavily speckled grayish-brown or pale yellow, together with webbing and slow plant growth. If it occurs, spray with malathion and give additional water and ventilation. Remember to allow the correct time interval between spraying and harvesting.

Halo blight: this is a seed-borne, bacterial disease which is encouraged by the practice of soaking the beans before sowing in wet seasons. The main symptoms are small, transparent spots which are surrounded by a yellow ring. Eventually the spots dry up, and where many are present, so that they coalesce, the entire leaf will wither. Seedlings may be killed outright, and even older plants can wilt completely. The pods can also be infected with round, moisture-oozing spots. Remove and destroy diseased plants as soon as seen. The best precaution is to only use seeds from reliable

sources; never sow seeds which are wrinkled or blistered or have yellow spots on them.

Anthracnose: this fungal disease is usually associated with cool, wet growing conditions. The main symptoms are dark brown elongated spots on the stems which result in the leaves withering. The pods can have small, round, sunken spots, reddish-brown in color, and the seeds inside diseased pods will eventually develop brownish-black markings. Spray with the currently approved fungicide in your area. The plants should be destroyed after cropping, and dwarf beans grown in a different place for several years. Because the disease is seed-borne, the best precaution against anthracnose is clean seed, obtained from a reliable source.

Root or foot rot: this fungal infection occurs most often on soils which are cold and badly drained. Roots growing in these conditions will be weakened, and thus will be more vulnerable to attack. Unfortunately, the symptoms of root rot are not visible above ground. If a plant is not growing well, and has yellow wilted foliage for no apparent reason, gently pry the soil away from the main stem. If root rot is the cause, then dark brown or reddish discolorations will be seen on the roots and base of the stems, and the roots will be withered looking. The crop is likely to be greatly reduced. As with all seed-borne diseases, the best precaution is to obtain clean seed from a reliable

GUIDE TO BEAN TROUBLES	
Symptoms	*Probable cause*
Seed leaves misshapen; seedlings stunted; small holes under surface skin of beans	Bean beetle
Irregular holes in leaves, stems and pods; faint silvery trails	Slugs
Stem cut off just above ground level	Cutworms
Plants, especially growing tips, covered in small black sucking insects	Bean aphid
Foliage eaten or skeletonized from below	Various beetles
Leaves speckled grayish brown or yellow; webbing present	Red spider mite
Small transparent spots with wide yellow rings around them, which later dry up; leaves withered	Halo blight
Dark brown spots on stems, reddish brown spots on pods	Anthracnose
Dark brown or reddish black spots on roots and base of stems; roots withered looking	Root rot
Fluffy gray mold on stems, leaves and pods	Botrytis
Leaves mottled dark green, light green and yellow; stunted plants, misshapen pods	Virus diseases
Plants weak, growing poorly in spite of favorable conditions	Nematodes

source. Affected plants should be destroyed after any crop has been taken. Those only slightly affected may be induced to throw out fresh roots by mulching up and around the stems.

Botrytis: this fungal infection, commonly called "gray mold," is usually associated with cold, wet growing conditions; seedlings are particularly vulnerable. As its common name implies, the main symptom is fluffy, gray mold appearing on the stems, leaves and, occasionally, pods.

Sufficient ventilation is important. In damp seasons especially, do not plant too close together. Spray with an approved fungicide, if necessary.

Virus: two diseases, common mosaic and yellow mosaic, occur on beans. The former produces dark and light green mottling, and distorted leaves. The plants are stunted and the crop reduced. Yellow mosaic produces yellow irregular patches on the green leaves, and the pods can be considerably misshapen. Common mosaic can be seed-borne; both are carried by aphids. As with all virus diseases, there is no remedy, and infected plants should be destroyed. Do not save seed for future sowing.

Varieties

A valuable crop for the home gardener, there are many varieties of beans.

Snap beans
Bountiful: a good, old sort; broad, flat, tasty. Ideal for French cutting.

Contender: vigorous plants with fairly large pods; stringless and tender. Resists mosaic, powdery mildew partially.

Goldcrop: All-American winner; erect, vigorous, disease-resistant. Pods round, stringless, straight. Use fresh, freeze, can.

Kinghorn Wax: a popular round-podded, white-seeded maincrop. Can or freeze.

Pencil Pod Wax: thick, round, meaty, prolific; tasty and brittle. Old but ever-popular.

Stringless Greenpod: tender, brittle and meaty; entirely stringless. Top flavor, round, productive.

Surecrop: a good, stringless wax with straight pods; stringless at all ages. Prolific, a "yellow Bountiful."

Improved Tendergreen: mosaic-resistant; pods round, smooth, free of strings. For table or freezing; yields well in hot weather.

Tendercrop: pods smooth, slender, dark green, straight; holds quality after picking. Resists mosaic.

Tenderette: delicately flavored, straight pods with white seeds; stay tender a long time; freeze well.

Topcrop: straight, medium green, bushy, vigorous. Resists mosaic; good canner and freezer.

Pole Beans
Blue Lake: straight, stringless, smooth, dark green; pods round, tender, meaty. A favorite for freezing and canning.

Scarlet Runner: an old favorite grown as much for colorful flowers as for beans. Pods tender and tasty, if harvested while young.

▲ *Bountiful*

Kentucky Wonder: the most popular pole bean; pods brittle, fibrous, long, bumpy.

Kentucky Wonder Wax: butter yellow, a bit later than green variety, otherwise much like it.

McCaslan: long-podded, round, fleshy, stringless. Quality good as either snap or shell beans.

Missouri Wonder: crops well even when others fail; pods long, tender. A good cornfield sort.

Romano (Italian Pole): heavy bearer of long, wide pods; green, stringless, meaty. Flavor distinctive; matures somewhat earlier than other pole varieties.

Striped Creaseback (Scotia): an old cornfield bean, still popular; pods purple-spotted, nearly stringless.

Shell beans
Garbanzo: also known as chick peas; small round, light brown beans. Eaten plain, in salads, and in Spanish and Oriental dishes.

Improved White Navy: a re-selected, very uniform strain; seeds smallish, white. Popular for baking.

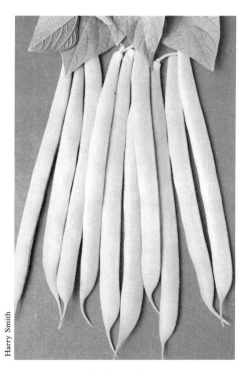
▲ *Contender*

⬆ *Left to right: Cyrus, Royalty, Goldcrop*

⬆ *Topcrop*

⬆ *Blue Lake*

⬆ *White Marrowfat*

French Horticultural Bush: produces some runners but not a climber; pods splashed red and yellow. Small beans frozen, larger eaten green, shell beans when mature.

Pinto: popular for re-fried beans, chili, etc.; pods short, broad, oval. Seeds light buff, speckled greenish brown.

White Marrowfat: seeds white, larger than navy beans; easier to shell, better for baking.

Red Kidney: seeds large, red, kidney-shaped. Hardy and high yielding.

Wren's Egg (Dwarf): pods greenish yellow splashed with red; prolific, medium late, stringless. Used as snap or shell beans.

Novelty bean
Royal Burgundy: pods purple, turn green after two minutes of boiling—a good blanching indicator; eat fresh or frozen. Round, tender; less attractive to beetles.

A New and Nourishing Bean

These beans have an extra-high protein content and are well worth trying in a warm garden. They can be dried and stored for use all winter in a variety of savory dishes.

Soybeans, also known as soya and soya beans, have more food value than most other legumes, and an extremely high protein content. The world's most extensively grown commercial crop, it is less often grown in gardens, although newer varieties now make it a worth while crop in warmer areas. It was introduced into the West relatively recently. There are over a thousand varieties of the plant, with brown, black, green or yellow beans. In appearance, the soybean plant is dense and hairy all over, with a trifoliate leaf pattern and short pods. The

▼ Soybeans of the variety Kanrich are a good choice for the home grower.

Brian Furner

purple or white flowers are not very noticeable. The pods are also hairy, and they contain between two and four beans.

Success with soybeans depends largely on the weather. They need a long, warm growing season, and they take about 100 days to mature—though they can be used earlier as green beans. Unlike other beans, the crop gets its signal for flowering from the length of the day, and most varieties have a particular, limited range of day-length in which they can mature properly and produce a satisfactory crop. Each group of varieties is adapted to a different narrow range of latitude, so it is important to choose a suitable variety.

Choose a sunny spot in the warmest part of the garden for your soybeans, preferably one which was manured for an earlier crop. The best soil is sandy and well-drained. Just before sowing, be sure to remove all weeds. The ground should be raked to a fine tilth.

Soybeans are not like other bean crops, so do not sow them in the same way. They are really a warm temperate to subtropical crop, so you must vary your sowing time according to the climate in your area.

In warm climates you can sow the seed in midspring. Sow 1¾ in (4 cm) deep at 6 in (15 cm) intervals in rows about 9 in (22.5 cm) apart. The seeds are quite large so you can space them carefully at sowing time to avoid thinning later. There should be no problem with germination, so long as the temperature is around

Harry Smith

⋏ *Young soybean plants growing strongly. The beans have not yet begun to form.*

70°F (21°C), and the first shoots should emerge in 5–10 days.

In cool climates, outdoor-sown seeds may not germinate readily, if sown too early, as a minimum soil temperature of 50°F (10°C) is necessary. If necessary, sow in a hotbed, cold frame or indoors, either in seed boxes or singly in 3 in (7.5 cm) pots. Keep them indoors on a sunny windowsill or in a warm green-house until germination. Plant out the seedlings when they are large enough to handle, spacing them as for seeds sown directly outdoors. The young plants may need to be protected unless the season is warm. A high night temperature in mid-summer (when the plants are flowering) is also needed for a successful crop.

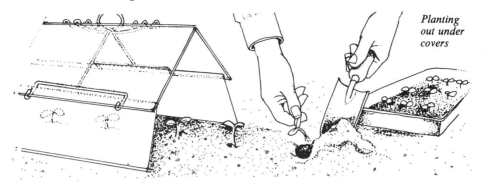

Planting out under covers

Adequate watering is essential for soybeans, as they will produce heavy crops only if the roots are always kept thoroughly moist. Always water profusely during a dry spell. A peat mulch applied just after sowing will help to retain necessary moisture, and it will also keep down weeds. Weeding can be a bit difficult with soybeans; you must never hoe too close to the plants or you could damage the shallow root system.

Although soybean plants can reach up to 6 ft (1.8 m) in tropical climates, they almost never grow more than 18–20 in (45–50 cm) tall in more temperate areas. Hence, staking is never necessary, as it is with most other beans.

Soybeans are troubled with very few pests or diseases. They can be infected by the fungus *Fusarium,* which causes the plants to wilt and eventually die. This trouble can be avoided by proper crop rotation; never grow soybeans on the same patch for two years in a row. Aphids can also be a nuisance, so keep a watch out for these pests and dust or spray with a nonpoisonous insecticide if necessary.

Your first soybeans should be ready for harvesting three or four months after sowing, depending on how favorable the weather has been. You can pick young, green pods and eat them whole, or you can let them mature. Older pods are ready for picking when they turn from green to dark yellow and when they begin to swell with the ripening beans. The best way to harvest mature beans is to pull up the whole plant, taking off all the pods at one time. To remove the beans, soak the pods in boiling water for five minutes, then crack them in half and squeeze out the beans.

Soybeans are perhaps most useful when stored and dried for winter use. To do this, lift the entire plant when the pods are yellow and hang them to dry in an airy, frost-free room. When the foliage is shrivelled and brittle, shell the beans. Spread the shelled beans in single layers on trays and dry them in a well-ventilated room. When thoroughly dry, store the beans in glass jars with loose-fitting lids. They will be ready for use in soups, stews and other nourishing dishes throughout the year.

Drying soybeans

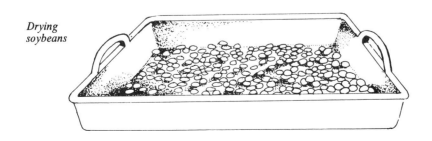

growing
ideas

Nutritious
Bean Sprouts

Ready to eat in a few days, effortless to grow and extremely nutritious, bean sprouts are as close as you can get to an instant vegetable.

Bean sprouts and seed sprouts are exceptional vegetables, unlike anything you grow in your garden. They are an indoor crop which can be started at any time of the year, and in any climate, since they require neither soil nor sun. And they are ready to eat in less than a week from the sowing date, sometimes in as little as three days. Because they are so quick and easy to grow, bean sprouts are an inexpensive and highly nutritious source of fresh vegetables all the year round. Extremely rich in vitamin C, they are delicious in salads and make an at-

Pat Brindley

▲ *Mung beans ready for harvesting (foreground); in the jar behind, germinating adzuki beans.*

Nutritious Bean Sprouts

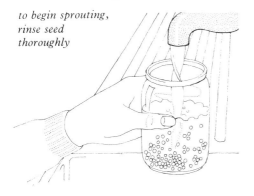

to begin sprouting, rinse seed thoroughly

drain jar; repeat four or five times

tractive and tasty addition to cooked dishes. They are also a familiar ingredient in many Chinese recipes and are used in curries and risottos.

The most popular beans for sprouting are mung beans and adzuki beans. Mung beans (*Phaseolus aureus*), also called Chinese bean sprouts, are pale green in color, with white sprouts. Adzuki beans (*Phaseolus angularis*) are rich mahogany-red beans, also with white sprouts. Other types include triticale, alfalfa and fenugreek, each with its own distinctive flavor.

Beans and seeds for sprouting can be obtained from specialty food stores, Chinese grocers and health food shops, as well as from seed merchants. Some suppliers offer "sprouting packs," containing several varieties of seeds and beans.

The simplest, cheapest and most effective way of growing bean sprouts is the glass jar method. All you need is a jam jar or a similar clear glass container, a rubber band and a piece of muslin. The muslin should be large enough to fit comfortably over the jar opening and be secured with the rubber band. If you do not have muslin, use a piece of cheesecloth, or any other fine, white cotton cloth.

If this is your first try at growing bean sprouts, do not exceed the recommended amount of seed. By the time the seed has sprouted and is ready to eat, it will have increased in volume as much as tenfold. If you start with too many seeds, they will fill up the jar and push out the top. With experience, you will learn the exact

quantity for your container and this will not happen.

Take about 2 teaspoons (10 ml) of the seed you plan to grow, and rinse it thoroughly in tepid tap water. The best way to do this is to place the seed in your glass jar, fill the jar nearly to the top with water, and shake vigorously. Drain completely, and then repeat the procedure four or five times, draining thoroughly after each rinse.

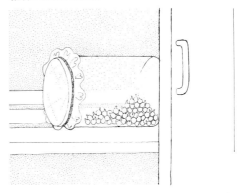

then place jar on its side in a dark cupboard

After rinsing several times, secure the muslin cover with the rubber band, and place the jar on its side in a dark cupboard. Temperature for sprouting must be between 55° and 65° F (12.7° and 18.3° C), so a pantry cupboard is an ideal place.

Bean sprouts are one of the most trouble-free crops you can grow. All that you need do is rinse the seeds thoroughly twice each day, morning and evening, then replace the jar in the dark place, al-

⋀ *Crisp and tender mung beans; harvest them when they are about 2 in (5 cm) long.*

ways on its side. The seeds must always be kept moist, but not really wet or they may go moldy.

You should notice your seeds beginning to sprout in a day or two. Mung beans will be ready to eat in three to five days, when they have increased in volume at least eight times, and the shoots are about 2 in (5 cm) long. Adzuki beans will be ready in four to six days, when the shoots have reached 1 in (2.5 cm). If you leave the beans to grow after they reach the desired length, they will become long and stringy, lose their crispness and discolor.

Bean seeds sprout because, with the help of warmth and moisture, the seeds' store of fats and starches are converted to vitamins, sugars and proteins for growth. Exactly the same process occurs when seeds are sown in soil. The sprouted seeds are highly nutritious and quite filling. Cook them quickly to retain the maximum vitamin content.

If you do not eat all the shoots at once, they will keep for a few days in the salad compartment of the refrigerator. However, as they are so cheap and easy to grow it makes sense to grow only what you can use at a single time, and then to start a new crop.

To start a second crop, simply wash and dry your container and start again with fresh seed.

Beets

Beta vulgaris (fam. *Chenopodiaceae*)
Half-hardy biennial, grown as an **annual**
Sowing to harvesting time: round and intermediate types 8–9 weeks; leaf and large types about 11 weeks
Size: plants about 1 ft (30 cm) tall, swollen roots between 1 in (2.5 cm) and 3½ in (9 cm) in diameter, according to form and variety at picking time
Yield: round and oval types, about 40 roots per 10 ft (3 m) row; leaf and large beet, about 30 roots per 10 ft (3 m) row

The beet is a fairly straightforward vegetable to raise, and one which has long been popular with amateur growers. It has so many uses in the kitchen that you are never likely to waste any of the crop—as well as adding rich color and flavor to soups, salads and relishes it is excellent served as a hot vegetable, and its high sugar content makes it a very good base for homemade wine.

The most common type of beet is round (sometimes called globe, or ball) and deep carmine in color. These are usually eaten in salads, when they are young and tender, but they can also be grown as a main crop and stored. There are two other shapes—oval (known as intermediate, or tankard) and long. Long beet is not often grown today, partly because some are less sweet and succulent than the round varieties, and partly because the roots are so large that they will not fit into today's modern saucepans. It does, however, store well and is good for exhibition work.

Although most varieties of beets are red, white and golden beets are now available to the amateur. These are round-shaped, and their main advantage over red beets is that they do not "bleed" in salads. They are doubly useful in the kitchen, because the leaves can be cooked and served like spinach.

By planting several varieties and giving some form of covered protection in early spring, you can easily have a good supply of beets nearly all the year round. A native of the Mediterranean region, it is not frost hardy in colder climates. Winter beets should be lifted before the ground freezes, and stored until you need them.

Suitable site and soil
Globe beets are reasonably tolerant of soil conditions, and will grow in any well-drained soil which does not dry out in summer. However, light sandy soils are ideal for all types of beets, particularly long varieties, which need a deep sandy loam to grow well. Select a site that is open and sunny for best results.

Begin preparing heavy soils in late autumn; light soils can be prepared early in spring. If the soil is very heavy, dig in plenty of half-rotted straw or peat to lighten it. Coarse sand can also be used. Double dig if you are preparing the bed for long beets, otherwise digging to about 7 in (17.5 cm) is adequate. Remove all weeds and their roots. If you have dug the soil in the autumn, leave it rough so that winter weather will break it down and make it more friable. If the soil is stony, remove as many as possible, because the roots should be able to grow and penetrate the soil without obstructions which may deform them.

Avoid adding fresh manure when preparing a bed for beets, or you are likely to get forked, misshapen roots. Ideally, beets should be grown on part of the vegetable plot which was manured the previous season; beets can sensibly follow celery, peas or pole beans. However, because of the beet's maritime associations, seaweed can be added to the soil, provided it is mixed into the bottom spit in autumn.

If the soil has an acid reaction, supply lime sometime in midwinter sufficient to make the pH neutral or very slightly alkaline. In spring, just before sowing, apply a complete fertilizer at the rate of 2 oz per sq yd (60 g per sq m), but only if seaweed was not added, and rake the soil level.

Sowing

Although beets are reasonably hardy, seedlings can be damaged by heavy frost. If the seedlings are not killed outright, they are liable to be stunted and produce seeds without forming an edible root. There is no point in sowing too early in the spring, unless you live in a very mild area or can give covered protection. For spring sowings, try to make a point of using bolt-resistant varieties, as beets have a great tendency to run to seed in dry and/or hot conditions.

Round beets for salads should be sown in small batches until midsummer. By monthly successional sowing, you will be provided with a continual supply of fresh young roots. Beets to be used for storage should be sown in early summer.

SOIL PREPARATION

1. **Prepare heavy soils in autumn, and leave rough over winter; light sandy soils can be prepared in the spring.**

2. **Test the soil; if it is acid, apply lime at a rate to give a neutral or slightly alkaline reaction (pH of 6.0–7.5).**

3. **In spring, work the soil to a fine tilth; prepare drills 1 ft (30 cm) apart and 1 in (2.5 cm) deep.**

SOWING AND THINNING

1. Sow seed clusters 2 in (5 cm) apart, in small batches, from midspring to midsummer.

2. After sowing, fill in the drills with fine soil and rake the bed lightly to give an even surface.

3. Thin the seedlings as soon as they are large enough to handle; leave one at each location.

4. Thin again, giving a final spacing of 4 in (10 cm) for round varieties, and 6 in (15 cm) for long varieties.

Do not sow them earlier, or they will have grown too coarse and woody by the time lifting starts in autumn.

Beet seeds are grouped in capsules, or clusters, each containing four or five seeds. Seeds, if properly stored, will maintain their viability for four years. To hasten germination, soak the seeds in water for a few hours before sowing. The average seed packet will contain enough seeds for several rows, so only soak as many as you intend to use immediately.

Sow each seed cluster 2 in (5 cm) apart in rows 1 ft (30 cm) apart. Make the drills 1 in (2.5 cm) deep, and after sowing fill in the drill with soil. Rake lightly to give a fine surface and water if the weather is dry. Germination should be within 12–24 days of sowing. When the seedlings appear, there will be clusters of them at each location. Remove all but the strongest as soon as they are large enough to handle. Thin them again, when they are between 1–3 in (2.5–7.5 cm) tall for round and intermediate varieties, and 6 in (15 cm) tall for long varieties, giving a spacing of 4 in (10 cm) and 6 in (15 cm) respectively.

CULTIVATION AND CARE

1. The beet needs a steady supply of water while it is growing, during the mid and late summer particularly.

2. Hoe as necessary between rows, being very careful not to damage the roots with the blade of the hoe.

3. For early beet crops, give some protection; remove covers during warm days and replace at night.

4. When harvesting, lift the roots carefully with a fork to avoid damaging the long taproot.

Care and development

The cultivation needs of the beet are moderate. For the best flavor, beets should grow quickly, otherwise tasteless, cracked, misshapen and tough roots will result. This means the plants must have a steady supply of water at the roots, especially during mid and late summer.

If you have thoroughly removed all weeds when preparing the soil, you should have little trouble with weeds while the crops are growing. Once the plants are established, they produce thick foliage which suppresses the weeds.

If weeding is necessary, however, hand weed between the plants to avoid damaging the roots; light hoeing between rows is all right if you are very careful and keep well away from the beets.

Because the beet in its natural state grows near the sea, a light application of agricultural (common or rock) salt is useful. Apply in early or midsummer, at the rate of 1 oz per sq yd (30 g per sq m) and fork it in lightly.

Birds are much attracted to seedlings and some protection is essential. You can protect the rows with netting, pea

▲ *Beet crops are best when grown quickly and given a steady supply of water.*

Harry Smith Collection

guards or black cotton thread twined around and through the leaves.

Forcing

Although you may have stored enough beets from the previous year's crop to last through spring, the fresh early beet is a real treat and one which is easy to produce. Round varieties are the most suitable for growing under covers or in frames. Tent and tunnel covers will accommodate a single row; wider sorts of covers will take two or three rows, spaced 7 in (17.5 cm) apart. Sow thinly in early spring in seed drills 1 in (2.5 cm) deep. Thin as soon as the seedlings are large enough to handle to 2 in (5 cm) apart; make sure they never run short of water.

After germination, provided that the days are not excessively cold, open the frames or covers slightly to admit air. Close when night temperatures fall below about 50° F (10° C). Remove the frame lid or covers entirely on days when temperatures average above 60° F (15.5° C), but replace in the evening if frost threatens.

Harvesting and storing

Round and intermediate varieties should be ready for pulling when they are about 1 in (2.5 cm) in diameter, about eight weeks after they are sown. These first pullings are in fact a form of thinning, as the remaining beets will have room to grow larger. For this reason, try to pick evenly over the rows, so the rest of the crop is reasonably spaced. These first pullings will be very tender, and useful for salads. Continue pulling more beets as and when needed, until they reach 2½–3 in (6.3–7.5 cm) in diameter. Try to pull the roots as soon as they are fully mature. Once the foliage begins to lose its fresh look and goes limp, it means that growing has stopped and the plants are best harvested immediately.

Main crops should be ready for harvesting from early autumn, continuing for about two months; this includes the long varieties for winter storing. Loosen the roots with a fork or spade and then lever out; it is best not to wrench the plants out by pulling the leaves. The one exception is the variety Formanova, which grows with most of the root out of the ground. These roots will come out quite easily when pulled by the leaves.

Do not cut off the leaves, but twist them off about 2 in (5 cm) above the crown. This is to avoid breaking the skin and subsequent bleeding, which would detract from the flavor and color. Then shake the root to remove adhering soil. The leaves of all varieties can be eaten fresh or cooked as greens.

All beets can be stored for future use; if properly stored they will keep until the first of the following year's crop is ready for lifting. Although some varieties are slightly more frost-hardy than others, beets can be damaged by severe frost. For this reason, unless you live in a very mild area, you should harvest the crop no later than the first skim of freezing soil. If you do leave them in the ground protect them from frost with a layer of clean straw or leaves. Select a dry day for lifting and be careful not to damage the roots in any way. Damaged, diseased or bruised roots cannot be stored as they may rot and quickly infect the others.

If your crop is moderate-sized, you can store it in boxes. Line the bottom of the container with 2 in (5 cm) of sand or peat; then lay the beets on the bottom, not touching each other. Add a 1 in (2.5 cm) layer of peat or sand and another layer of beets and so on until the box is fully packed. Then store the boxes in a dry frost-free place such as a garden shed, garage or cellar. If the storage conditions are too warm or moist, the roots may continue to grow or rot may set in and spoil the crop.

If your harvest is a large one and you live in an area where they can be protected from freezing, you can build a clamp, similar to a potato clamp, for beet storage.

Container growing

Choose round varieties for container growing. Large tubs are most suitable

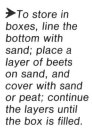

➤*To store in boxes, line the bottom with sand; place a layer of beets on sand, and cover with sand or peat; continue the layers until the box is filled.*

GROWING LONG BEETS FOR EXHIBITION

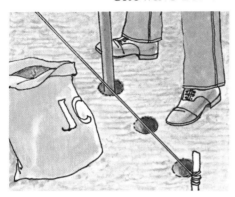

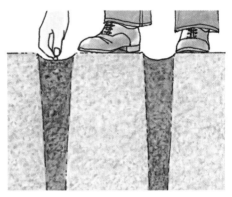

1. Make holes with a crowbar 3½ ft (1.05 m) deep, and 1 ft (30 cm) apart. Leave 1½ ft (45 cm) between rows.

2. Fill the holes with a good, friable potting mixture; press the mix in firmly, and sow seeds in the top.

but, if using pots, the smallest useful size is 12 in (30 cm). Fill the bottom 2 in (5 cm) of the container with small pieces of broken bricks, pieces of flower pot or gravel to provide drainage. Fill the container with a good, friable, well-drained potting mixture to within 2 in (5 cm) of the rim. Then sprinkle the seeds thinly over the surface and cover with another 1 in (2.5 cm) of the mix. Water well, using a fine rose on the watering can. Thin the seedlings to allow enough room for them to develop, leaving only eight plants in a 12 in (30 cm) diameter pot. Water frequently in warm weather.

▲ *Round varieties are the best sort for container growing; keep them well watered.*

Brian Furner

Exhibition tips

Try to time the beet sowing so the crop will be just ready for exhibiting; roots which are premature or those which are old and woody will not win prizes. For early summer shows, long varieties should be sown in early spring outdoors with glass protection. Globe varieties should be sown in midspring for midsummer shows, and in late spring for late summer shows.

Globe roots for show can be selected from ordinary crops, and no special cultivation is needed. Long varieties for show are best planted in holes made by a crowbar, 1 ft (30 cm) apart, 3½ ft (1.05 m) deep, in rows 18 in (45 cm) apart, filled with potting mixture. Press the mix in firmly, leaving a 1 in (2.5 cm) depression in the top, in which the seeds are sown. Thin out to one strong plant as soon as the seedlings are large enough to handle, and continue cultivating as for normal crops.

When it is time to lift the roots, either round or long, you must take care not to damage the taproot. Do not pull the plants out of the ground by their leaves; it is much better to lift them with a fork or spade.

For both varieties, remove the tiny side rootlets with a sharp knife. Cut off all the outer leaves cleanly; leave 3 in (7.5 cm) of leaf stalk from the inner leaves. Wash the roots in cold water to

3. Before the show, trim back leaf stalks to 3 in (7.5 cm) and cut off tiny rootlets with a sharp knife.

remove any soil adhering, but do not scrub them. Dry the roots and wrap them in paper until the show.

Very large roots are not necessarily prize winners; it is best to select medium-sized roots which have good color and are free from blemishes, pale inner rings and damage. The taproot should still be intact. Globe varieties should be symmetrical, smooth skinned, and about the size of a tennis ball. Long varieties should taper evenly from the shoulder to a single taproot. Do not enter roots which are forked or have gall marks, or roots which bulge too much in the middle.

Long varieties are usually shown in a flat basket on a bed of parsley; round varieties can be piled, pyramid shape, in a round basket. Just before judging, spray the beets with a fine mist of water, to make them as visually appetizing as possible.

Pests & Diseases

Keep in mind that you can control many beet-growing problems with nonchemical preventive measures. They include use of fungicide-treated seeds, frequent hoeing around plants, avoidance of overcrowded seedlings, keeping gardens free of weeds and debris, and correcting a too-limy soil before planting.

Mangold flies (beet leaf miner): the maggots of the mangold fly damage the leaves of beets by feeding on them; they mine through the leaves and produce large, pale brown blisters. The worst damage is done when the plants are young; in bad attacks the plants may be killed outright. Infested plants will be stunted; leaves will turn completely brown, wither and die. Pick off and burn all infested leaves. If it is a severe attack, spray the remainder with malathion. Remember to allow the specified interval to elapse between treatment and harvesting. It is a good idea to apply a quick-acting fertilizer to attacked crops to give them a chance to make fresh top growth.

Beet carrion beetle: the grub and adult stage of this black beetle feed on the tender leaves for about three weeks in spring; in severe attacks, the plants may be killed. In general it is not a serious pest, and clean cultivation and frequent hoeing are the best preventive measures. If your plants are attacked, spray with derris as soon as the pests are seen and repeat as necessary.

Sphinx moth: the large caterpillars of these moths can be very destructive; they pupate in the soil and feed on the roots. Hoe and fork lightly round the beets reg-

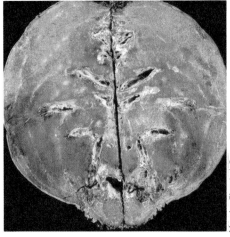

Murphy Chemical Co.

▲ *Crown or heart rot is an indication of boron deficiency; roots get cankered and black.*

ularly if the soil is infested; this will kill some caterpillars and expose some to insect-eating birds. Because they also feed on the roots of many weeds, try to keep your garden weed free. If the attack is severe, try malathion.

Scab: this fungal disease is usually associated with limy soils. Symptoms are small marks or sunken pits; occasionally they are raised above the level of the skin. The small markings will gradually increase in size, until the whole root is disfigured. Although plants are rarely killed by scab, any beet covered with scab is less pleasant to eat. The best preventive measure is to correct the pH of the soil before planting. You can also dig in green manure, lawn mowings, or moist peat just before sowing as an additional precaution.

Damping-off: this is a fungal disease associated with wet, overcrowded conditions. Infected seedlings will collapse at ground level and die; roots of infected plants are usually discolored reddish-brown. The best preventive measure is to avoid overcrowding the seedlings; thin as soon as they are big enough to handle. If the seedlings are attacked, remove and destroy the infected plants and spray the remainder with a solution of captan or zineb.

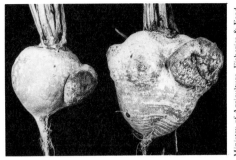

Crown gall is a bacterial infection which causes bumps to form on the sides of roots.

Ministry of Agriculture, Fisheries & Food

Violet root rot: this is a very serious fungal disease. It is soil-borne, and infected roots when lifted will show webs of violet strands enmeshing them. The above-ground symptoms of violet root rot are wilting and yellow leaves, but to be absolutely sure you must dig up and inspect the root of the suspect plant. Unfortunately, there is no chemical cure; grub up and destroy infected plants. Do not replant the site with beets, or any other vegetable susceptible to violet root rot for several years. Parsnip, carrots, asparagus and potatoes are particularly susceptible, so avoid planting them if the soil is infected.

Beet rust: this is a less severe fungal infection, the symptoms of which are small red-brown spots on the under surfaces of

GUIDE TO BEET TROUBLES

Symptoms	Probable causes
Brown, withered and blistered leaves	Leaf miner
Leaves eaten	Beet carrion beetle
Roots eaten	Sphinx moth caterpillar
Small marks or sunken pits on roots; roots disfigured	Scab
Seedlings collapse and die	Damping-off
Yellow stunted leaves; roots surrounded by webs of violet fungus	Violet root rot
Small brown spots on leaves	Beet rust
Large hollow cavities in roots	Crown gall
Blackened root and central leaves	Boron deficiency
Pale areas between leaf veins which eventually turn brown and die	Magnesium deficiency
Yellow blotches on leaves; leaves curled upward	Manganese deficiency

Murphy Chemical Co.

↟ *These beets are infected with scab, a fungal disease associated with limy soils.*

Ministry of Agriculture, Fisheries & Food

↟ *Beets suffering from manganese deficiency have discolored or curled leaves.*

the leaves. It is most likely to be seen in autumn and is unlikely to cause much trouble. Pick off and burn infected leaves as soon as you see them; if the disease is severe, spray the remainder with captan or zineb. Spray again two weeks later.

Crown gall: this is a bacterial infection usually associated with badly drained soils. The bacteria enter the plant through a wound, perhaps made by an insect or damage from a hoe or fork. Once inside the roots, their attack results in the formation of large bumps on the sides of the roots. It is not a serious infection, although the roots may be slightly stunted and less appetizing. However, many other root plants can be seriously attacked and damaged, so infected roots should be dug up and burned as soon as seen. The best preventive measure is to correct any drainage problems before the crop is planted; also avoid damaging the roots during routine cultivation.

Boron deficiency: this is most likely to occur on light sandy soils in dry weather; plants growing on very limy soils are also vulnerable. The symptoms of boron deficiency are commonly called crown or heart rot; the central leaves die back and become blackened, and the roots may turn black on the inside and be cankered on the outside. To correct boron deficiency, mulch with plenty of garden compost, well-rooted manure, leafmold, or seaweed, or apply liquid seaweed fertilizer at the recommended rate.

Magnesium deficiency: magnesium is one of the constituents of chlorophyll, and if beets are lacking magnesium, pale areas will appear between the leaf veins. Eventually these discolored areas turn brown and die. The deficiency is most likely to occur on very acid or very limy soils, but in general it is seldom encountered. One or more foliar sprays at two-weekly intervals with magnesium sulfate (Epsom salts) at the rate of 2 oz in 1 gal (60 g in 4.5 L) of water may be tried. A good mulch of well-rotted garden compost should help with the problem in the long term, and also heavy dressings of bulky organic matter when winter digging will gradually eliminate it. On very acid soils, an application of lime is helpful. Alternatively, if such manures are not available, Dolomite or magnesium limestone can be applied in winter to acid soils, at the rate of 7 oz per sq yd (210 g per sq m).

Manganese deficiency: the disease called "speckled yellows" which also appears on spinach, is really a symptom of manganese deficiency. Affected plants have leaves with yellow blotches between the veins, and the leaves tend to curl up, usually in midsummer. Both very sandy and very alkaline soils can be deficient in manganese. Some natural recovery can occur; the long varieties seem much less susceptible. In severe cases, apply a foliar spray of manganese sulfate at the rate of 2 oz in 5 gal (60 g in 22.5 L) of water with a few drops of liquid detergent.

Varieties

Boltardy: 60 days. New, similar to Detroit Dark Red. Sweet, fresh flavor; ringless and totally without fiber. Extremely resistant to bolting.

Burgundy: 59 days. Sweet and deep red throughout. Tops stronger, taproots smaller than most beets; particularly good for pickling.

Cherry or Eclipse: 44 days. Oval with a dark red color; fine-grained, tender and well-flavored. Practically free of side roots; very early. Good for exhibition.

Crosby's Egyptian: 48 days. Semi-globe to heart-shaped; quality good. A desirable very early sort; long a favorite for quick cropping.

Detroit Dark Red: 58 days. Perhaps best known and an old favorite variety; ideal for growing on muck, peat or rich upland soils. Deeply colored, ringless; exceptionally sweet and tender.

Early Wonder: 55 days. Quick, uniform, smooth-skinned beet for the table, pickling or canning. Semi-globe, medium-topped, dark red with lighter zones.

King Red: 63 days. An outstanding canning type; similar to Detroit Dark Red but rounder and with redder interior.

Mono Germ: 45 days. Much like Detroit but produces one sprout per seed instead of several as do most beets, thereby eliminating most of need for thinning.

▲ *Detroit*

Mono King Explorer: 62 days. Like Mono Germ, produces only one plant per seed; smooth, sweet-flavored and deep-colored.

Red Ball: 60 days. Tasty, sweet, dark red flesh without zones or fiber; retains color in cooking. Uniformly globe-shaped, convenient moderate size.

Redpak: 61 days. Noted for vigorous, short tops and uniformly round shape; little or no zoning. A good canner; suited to high land, sandy soils.

Ruby Queen: 60 days. A leading canner in Northeast; smooth, uniformly round. Tops small and green; fine taproots. Deep red and free of zoning.

▼*Formanova*

▼*Early Wonder*

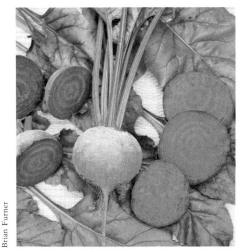

▲ *Ruby Queen*

▲ *Burpee's Golden*

Novelty and unusual varieties

Albino: 50 days. Green tops good for cooking; globe-shaped, sweet, fairly smooth; novel color prevents bleeding in salads, canning, table use, or pickling.

Burpee's Golden: 50 days. A good dual-purpose beet; use tops in salad or like spinach, roots in usual ways. Cannot bleed. A fast grower for early sowing and succession planting.

Formanova (Improved Cylindrica): 58 days. A carrot-shaped, high-quality beet, providing many and uniform slices; inside rich red, free of zoning. Formanova has a tendency to push out, hill to prevent sun scalding.

Long Season (Winter Keeper): 78 days. Makes very large roots that are tender regardless of size. Tops good for greens; roots store well in sand.

Lutz Greenleaf: 80 days. Roots half-long, top-shaped; inside dark red with lighter zones. Good small or large; stay sweet all summer. Stores well.

Snowhite: 62 days. Crisp, icy-white; cannot smudge or bleed. Served hot or cold, flavor excellent; leaves make good greens, raw or cooked.

Tendersweet: 55 days. Early, cylindrical; excellent for slicing. Very sweet and tender at all stages. Stalks also sweeter than most beets; make good greens.

➤*Crosby's Egyptian*

Blackberries

Species of *Rubus* (fam. *Rosaceae*) mainly derived from R. *fruticosus,* which itself has been subdivided into many species
Hardy perennial cane, usually prickly, with a cropping life of about 15 years
Planting to harvesting time: two years
Size: 6 ft (1.8 m) in height and up to 15 ft (4.5 m) wide when trained flat
Yield: about 5–10 lb (2.25–4.5 kg) per plant under favorable conditions

Shiny, sweet and flavorful, blackberries are among the easiest of cane fruits to grow. They will thrive in almost any soil, and will produce good crops even when grown in heavy shade. Because they flower late and over a long period, frost does not bother them at all; even if some flowers are killed by late frosts, more will be produced. Although birds may take the occasional berry, they are not generally troublesome and there is no need for blackberries to be grown in a fruit cage.

Blackberries used to have a reputation for being awkward and difficult garden plants because of their over-vigorous growth, which quickly swamps neighboring fruits and vegetables. Also, annual pruning, which is necessary if the plants are to crop at all well, was regarded as a formidable and often painful task because of the numerous wicked thorns which cover the canes. Luckily, plant breeders have solved both of these problems. There are several new varieties with moderate growth habits available and these are eminently suitable for smaller gardens. Secondly, thornless varieties have been developed which make pruning easier.

Blackberries have not been widely cultivated because in suburban and rural areas bramble patches were so abundant and, in good years, the fruit plentiful. However, there are far fewer such patches today than in the past, due to intensive farming methods and increased residential construction. Some people still prefer the slightly acid taste of the wild blackberry, but cultivated varieties tend to have larger berries and heavier crops.

Suitable site and soil
Blackberries are very accommodating with regard to site and soil; indeed, they can often be grown in dark corners where nothing else will grow. However, if you want first class crops, then some care must be taken in selecting a site and

G. E. Hyde

▲ *Blackberries will grow in shade, and are ideal for training against a north-facing fence.*

preparing the soil. Unlike strawberries, replaced every three years or so, blackberries can have a useful life of ten to fifteen years or more, making initial choice of site particularly important.

It should be reasonably sheltered from north and east winds and, although the blackberry is a shade-tolerant plant, crops will be heavier if full sun is available. Low-lying land or land subject to frost is no problem because blackberries flower very late in spring or perhaps early summer and even a late frost will do little harm. Flowers will continue to appear for a while if earlier ones are killed.

Well-drained medium to heavy loams are ideal; light or sandy soils need addi-

tional organic matter dug in. Whatever the soil type, it must be moisture retentive; if the plants run short of water in summer, hard, small berries will result. A limestone soil is least suitable, and if you want to attempt blackberries on such a soil, then plenty of manure must be dug in before planting. Depending on the quality of the existing soil, add between 5–15 lb per sq yd (2.5–6.5 kg per sq m). Ideally, the soil should be slightly acid, with a pH of 6.5–6.8. Test your soil, and take whatever corrective measures are necessary. As a general rule, thorny varieties of blackberries are stronger than thornless ones. If your soil is not first class, or the only spot left in your garden is a shady one, select a strong-

Step-by-step Growing Guide for Blackberries

TRAINING WIRES

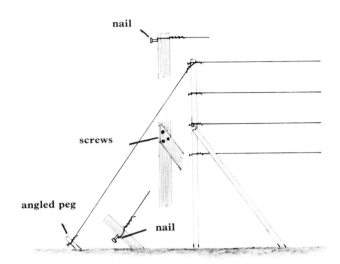

nail

screws

angled peg

nail

Metal, wooden, or concrete posts make suitable supports for training wires. There should be 6 ft (1.8 m) of post above ground. Make wires 1 ft (30 cm) apart, starting 3 ft (90 cm) above ground. Use struts or guy wires at end posts to give additional strength.

growing variety. You will still get reasonably good harvests, and the growing conditions will restrict the excessive cane and leaf growth.

Make sure the site is free from perennial weeds before planting, as once the canes are in, weed eradication will be difficult. Remember, too, that unless you select a thornless variety, the long sharp thorns on the canes can make for painful scratches if they are planted near a much-used path or doorway, so try to keep blackberries well away from the central part of your garden. In fact, they make excellent boundary planting for this very reason.

Training wires and fences

If you are erecting wire fences to support the canes, do this before planting. You can use metal, wooden, or concrete posts. Wood posts should be treated with a preservative so that the buried portion does not rot. Galvanized piping can be used for the uprights, although this form of support presents problems when it comes to attaching wires. Store-bought metal or concrete posts usually have holes drilled through them at 1 ft (30 cm) intervals.

The posts should be 7½ ft (2.3 m) tall, with 6 ft (1.8 m) above the ground. Re-

member that fully grown plants will be very heavy and if you skimp on your support system, you may find that a bad storm will cause plants, posts and wires to collapse.

Use ⅛ in (3 mm) plastic coated wires, or else insulated telephone wire. Alternatively, agricultural pig fencing can be used. The wires should be 1 ft (30 cm) apart, starting 3 ft (90 cm) above the ground. Try to attach the wire ends to straining eyes, so that any subsequent sagging can be easily corrected. Intermediate struts between the main posts will help in this respect, too. The end posts should be propped with additional struts, or you can run guy ropes from the top of the post outward to a well-secured peg.

On a wall, fence or shed, the same spacing between wires should be used. Secure the wires by fixing them to vine eyes or spikes which have been hammered into the brick or wood.

Planting out

The best time to plant is early spring in the North, provided the soil is not waterlogged or frozen. The distance between plants varies a great deal, according to the strength of the variety. If you are uncertain about a particular variety, ask at

PLANTING

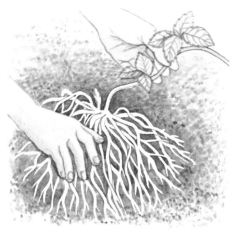

1. In early spring, dig planting hole 4–5 in (10–12.5 cm) deep; spread roots well out so they are fully extended.

2. Cover with soil and firm lightly; cut the old cane back to 9 in (22.5 cm). If the soil is dry, water well.

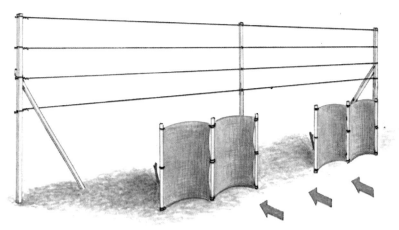

3. Provide temporary protection from strong winds until plants are settled in, and again every year when plants are in full flower.

your nursery or garden center for specific planting distances.

Whatever the variety, if you are planting more than one row, leave at least 6 ft (1.8 m) between them. This not only allows you to prune and harvest easily but permits sunlight to reach the plants, which is necessary for new growth to be hardened properly and for the berries to become fully ripened.

Dig the planting hole 4–5 in (10–12.5 cm) deep. Cut off broken roots and set the plants in with the roots spread out

naturally to their full length. The crown should be level with the soil surface. Crumble the soil over the roots, firming it gently as you go, until the soil is level with that surrounding it. If the soil is dry, give the newly planted canes a thorough watering.

After planting, cut down the canes to 9 in (22.5 cm). Although this precludes fruiting the first year, it will encourage the roots to settle in and produce healthy future growth. If you leave the canes uncut, the first year's crop will be poor

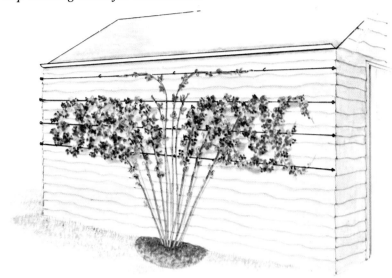

Space wires on wall, fence or shed 1 ft (30 cm) apart; fix them to vine eyes or spikes hammered into wood or bricks.

and it will take several years for the plant to recover fully, if it does so at all, from the strain of premature fruiting.

Training

Blackberries need exposure to as much light and air as possible, and the various systems of training are all based on this. Following is an ideal procedure for training them. This may be followed completely or to whatever extent the home gardener wishes. Basically, the current year's shoots are kept tied in and separate from the older fruiting shoots; the young shoots are trained upright with the fruiting canes radiating out on either side of them. When the fruiting canes have finished cropping, they are cut away completely, and the young canes are retied to take their place. The center is then left empty, and ready to be filled by the following year's new canes. This may sound a bit overwhelming, but it is not at all difficult.

Do not be tempted to allow your blackberries to grow unpruned and untrained. Overgrown blackberry thickets usually have only dead or diseased wood in the center, with the healthy fruiting canes on the outside where light and air are available. Growing blackberries in this way is a waste of space that very few gardens can afford today.

During the first summer after planting, usually only one or two canes will grow, and these will not fruit. Wearing stout gloves as protection against thorns, gradually tie them up and along the top or nearest suitable wire. Late the following winter, check the canes for dieback or frost damage, and remove any dead wood. If the canes have grown too vigorously for the space allotted them, cut them back by about 2–4 ft (60–120 cm), and any sideshoots to within a hand span of the main stem. Early next summer, begin training them along the wires provided.

Although there will only be a couple of fruiting canes the first season, from the second summer onwards there should be 8–10 canes per plant.

There are several patterns of training, but the simplest is to weave the fruiting canes between the bottom and third wire (see diagram), leaving the center empty for new canes. Choose the two canes neares: the center and take them up to the second top wire and attach them one on either side, leaving the center empty, with about a 2½ ft (75 cm) space be-

TRAINING

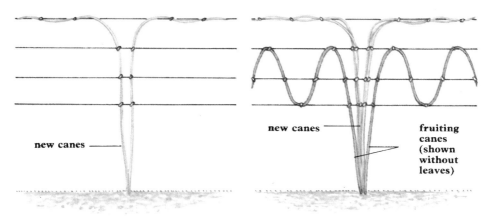

1. The first summer after planting, only one or two canes are produced; tie them up and along top wire.

2. Untie and begin training these canes along wires the following summer; tie new shoots as before.

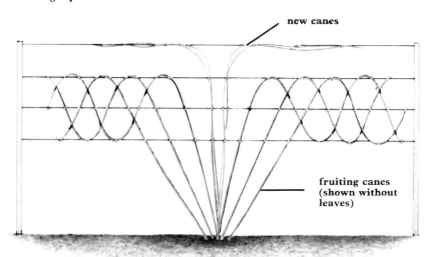

3. Established plants have eight to ten fruiting canes; start with middle pair of canes and weave along wires; leave center empty for new canes.

Alternative weaving patterns: dotted lines indicate new growth which will fruit next year; solid lines show this year's fruiting canes. Spacing depends on vigor of variety grown.

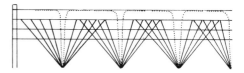

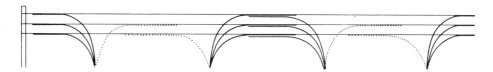

CULTIVATION AND CARE

1. Top dress plants in early summer with well rotted manure or garden compost 1 in (2.5 cm) thick.

2. If the weather is dry while the fruits are forming, water with a perforated hose laid along rows.

3. Begin harvesting in midsummer; pick over the canes every few days, to encourage more fruit to ripen.

tween them. Now weave them down to the bottom wire and up again, working outward from the middle. Tie the canes to the wires with strong garden twine or plastic-covered wire as you proceed. Now take the second pair of canes up to the second top wire, about 9 in (23 cm) outside the first pair, then repeat, and so on, until all the canes are tied in.

Each summer, as new shoots are produced, tie them vertically up the middle, and when they reach the top wire, spread them out on either side and tie them along the top wire to stop them from whipping about.

Pruning

There are two periods during the year when pruning is normally carried out: immediately after cropping, and in late winter. When cropping has finished, cut out the canes which have fruited, either completely or to the strongest new shoot low on a cane. It is far better to use new shoots growing directly from the ground, though, and only use canes growing from old wood if there are not enough new ones.

Summer pruning of the old canes is a much easier chore if two people work at it, so if you can get someone to help you with this task, so much the better. One person can then do the actual cutting, while the other takes and gathers up the prunings from the plant and moves them to the bonfire.

Untie the new canes and disentangle them if necessary. Lay them out singly on the ground and divide them equally into two groups. It is usual to retain only 8–10 canes on each plant. These are then tied in the pattern previously described.

In late winter or early spring, check the new canes for dieback or excessively

CULTIVATION AND CARE

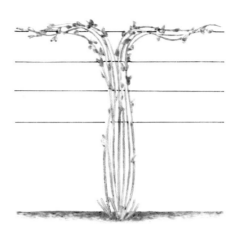

1. Check thornless varieties for thorny suckers. Cut them off below ground, where they join the root.

2. In autumn, after fruiting is over, cut old canes down to ground level. Clear them away and burn them.

3. Untie and spread out new canes. Retain 8-10 canes and train out for fruiting.

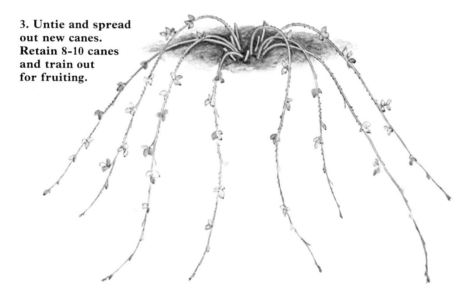

vigorous growth and prune accordingly. This is the best time to inspect the new canes springing from the base of thornless varieties. Occasionally, these plants revert and send out canes with thorns. Thorny canes tend to be stronger-growing than thornless ones and would, if given a chance, quickly overwhelm the weaker thornless types. Dig out these suckers, and cut them off below ground where they join the main roots.

Cultivation and care
You should provide temporary protection from strong winds until the plants are established, and again, every year, when the plants are in full flower. If it is too windy at this time, insects will be less likely to visit the flowers and adequate pollination may not take place.

In the summer months while the fruits are forming, water if the weather is dry. The best method is a perforated hose

Donald Smith

▲ *Good crops of blackberries ready for picking; for preserving, select firm, ripe berries.*

laid along each side of the row in turn. In a normal year, watering increases the yield; during a drought it is doubly vital. If water runs short not only will the berries be hard and small, but the production of new canes will suffer. Since next year's fruit will be produced on these canes, weak stunted canes will mean poor future crops.

Top-dress the plants every year in early summer with well-rotted manure or garden compost 1 in (2.5 cm) thick. If this is not available, use a complete fertilizer and mulch with straw. If the soil is dry, water thoroughly before mulching and the mulch will help conserve soil moisture as well as keeping weeds down.

Harvesting
Because fruit is produced on the previous year's wood, there will be no crop the first year. Depending on the varieties planted, cropping starts in midsummer from the second season onwards.

As with raspberries, avoid picking the fruit in rainy weather. Mold forms on wet blackberries very quickly. If you have to pick wet berries, eat or preserve them as soon as possible. Blackberries for freezing, jam-making and bottling should be picked when ripe, but slightly firmer than those used fresh for dessert.

To encourage more fruit to ripen, pick over the canes every few days, or even daily for heavy-cropping types. Overripe berries are particularly vulnerable to insect infestation, as well as fungal and viral infections, so make sure you remove and destroy any you find.

Preserving
Select firm, plump, fully ripe blackberries with glossy skins. Green berries may cause off-flavor. Sort and remove any leaves and stems

Using cold water, wash a small quantity at a time to save undue handling which may bruise delicate fruits such as blackberries. A perforated or wire basket is useful. Lift washed fruits out of the water and drain thoroughly. Don't let them stand in water—they can lose food

PROPAGATION

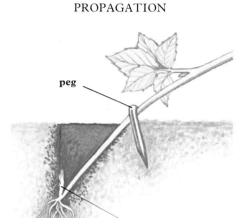

peg

new shoot

Blackberries are easily propagated by tip-layering. Make a hole 6 in (15 cm) deep; insert tip, and cover with soil.

value and flavor that way, or get water-soaked. When the blackberries have drained, proceed to freeze, can or make jam.

Propagation

As with raspberries, propagation of blackberries is easy but risky. This is because diseases infecting the parent plant will almost certainly be transmitted to the new stock. Virus infections, particularly, can make the whole exercise a waste of time because there are no symptoms in the earliest stages of infection and seemingly healthy parent plants may be infected. It is safest not to propagate new canes from your own fruiting stock, but instead buy in fresh stock.

If you do want to propagate blackberries, it is most easily done by tip-layering in summer. When the new canes are long enough to be bent over to the ground without snapping they are ready for layering. Make a hole a hand span deep; if the soil is at all heavy, it pays to dig some of it out and replace with friable loam or compost. If the soil is dry, water it thoroughly before inserting the tip. This should be buried about 6 in (15 cm) deep in the soil, at an angle of 45°, and held in place by a wooden peg or bent wire so that it does not spring out (see

diagram). The new plants should be well rooted by late autumn, but it is best to delay moving them until early spring, when they can be transplanted to their permanent position. To do this, sever the cane about 1 ft (30 cm) from the tip, and lift the young plant carefully with a spade or shovel so that the roots are damaged as little as possible. Cut back the remainder of the parent cane to ground level.

Blackberry plants occasionally throw up suckers, sometimes some distance from the parent plant. The best time to propagate from suckers is during the autumn. Gently loosen the rooted suckers and then sever them from the parent plant with a sharp spade. Make sure the suckers have strong, healthy root systems and discard any which are weak or spindly. Plant the suckers out in their permanent positions, and immediately cut them back to 9 in (22.5 cm) above ground.

Exhibition tips

Blackberries are not often seen at summer shows, perhaps because not too many people grow them. Secondly, many blackberry varieties are unlikely to be ripe for the early and midsummer shows, and a cold, wet summer can mean that no blackberries will be ripe for the late summer shows either. However, no special cultivation requirements are necessary and, if the weather has been reasonable, well cared for canes should have plenty of berries up to show standard.

Thirty blackberries is a common number required. Leave the picking to the last possible moment, so that the berries arrive at the show bench as fresh as possible. Select twice the number required, so you will have plenty of replacements, should you need them. Cut the berries, leaving about 1 in (2.5 cm) of the stalk attached.

Display the berries in a single layer in a shallow plate or dish. The judges will look for large fruits, fully ripe and well colored, without any blemishes, and with stalks intact.

Varieties

Bailey: a good midseason berry but not quite up to Darrow in many places; susceptible to rust.

Brazos: originated in Texas for warm climate; very early, large berries. For processing, eating fresh.

Darrow: probably best northern type at present; berries large, top quality, productive. Long season.

Early Harvest: good, medium-sized berries; good from Cape Cod south, midwest. Rust-susceptible.

Eldorado: midseason, firm, good quality; originated in Ohio.

Hedrick: early, large, medium firm; Geneva (N.Y.) Experiment Station.

Jerseyblack: midseason, large, good quality; vigorous, semi-trailing. Productive but thorny.

Thornfree: medium large, semi-firm, semi-acid; earlier than Darrow, nonsuckering, from U.S. Department of Agriculture.

▲ Darrow

McDonald: very early, semi-trailing, good quality; from Texas, for South.

Other varieties

Merton Early: sweet, shiny berries with very few seeds; very compact early grower, suitable for smaller gardens; heavy cropper.

Bedford Giant: large black fruit; excellent flavor; heavy early cropper but not suitable for growing in cold or exposed

▲ Thornfree

▲ Jerseyblack

Step-by-step Growing Guide for Blackberries

areas; fairly vigorous growth; berries have very few seeds and are suitable for jam-making or eating fresh; picking lasts for about a month.

Himalayan Giant: large fruit; flavor moderate and slightly acidic; very strong midseason grower with exceedingly spiky canes; old canes will continue bearing fruit for several years.

Oregon Thornless (Thornless Evergreen): vigorous midseason grower with thornless canes; leaves of the parsley type; berries have excellent flavor; needs good soil to do well, but will thrive in northern gardens.

Merton Thornless: good midseason cropper with medium size, fine-flavored fruit; needs good soil to crop well; moderately vigorous growth.

Cut-leaved Blackberry (Parsley-leaved): form of English wild blackberry with dark red canes and deeply cut leaves; midseason type with large berries of excellent flavor, vigorous only in good conditions; leaves have attractive autumn coloring.

John Innes: late type heavy cropper, with excellent flavored large berries, few seeds; continues cropping over several weeks; growth vigorous but not suitable for cold sites; less prickly than most.

Pests & Diseases

The blackberry is a plant native to temperate climates and is relatively free of troubles. In the list that follows the ones most likely to appear are redberry mite (redberry disease) and rust. As with other fruits, at some point you will probably need to use a chemical control to be sure of a good blackberry crop. Follow label directions for application of chemicals carefully, making certain to note the time for discontinuance in advance of harvesting. Another control is the burning of diseased canes and plants to prevent the spread of infections.

Redberry mite: these pests are the cause of what is commonly called "redberry disease"; hybrid berries, such as loganberries, are also vulnerable. The tiny mites spend winters beneath the bud scales on the canes; once the leaves have opened, the mites form colonies on the undersides where they feed and breed. The flowers are also attacked, and fruits of infested plants will be misshapen and unevenly ripened. Some of the drupelets never color properly, but remain bright red. This is primarily a difficulty on the West Coast, but is not as serious as it once was.

The best precaution is to burn old canes as soon as they have finished fruiting, so the mites will be unable to spend the winter in the garden. If you have had

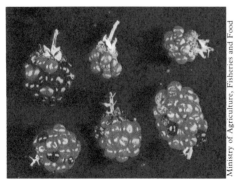

Ministry of Agriculture, Fisheries and Food

▲ *Redberry mite: infested berries do not ripen properly, but remain bright red in color.*

Royal Horticultural Gardens, Wisley

▲ *Larva of the raspberry beetle feeding on a blackberry; a problem abroad.*

trouble with the redberry mite in previous years, apply a summer oil emulsion in late fall.

Aphids: there are several species of aphid which infest blackberries, but the symptoms and control of all of them are very similar. Besides physically weakening the plants, they may transmit viral diseases and for this reason, every effort must be made to eliminate these pests from your garden.

They are most damaging in late spring and early summer; they suck the sap from the leaves, which then become curled and stunted. If you have had serious problems with aphids, apply a midwinter spray of dormant oil wash to kill any overwintering eggs. Otherwise, if they do appear in spring, spray with rotenone or malathion before the flowers open, and repeat if necessary. Avoid spraying the plants while they are in full flower; remember to allow the specified time to elapse between spraying and harvesting.

Botrytis cinerea (gray mold): blackberries growing in very cold, wet conditions are most vulnerable to this fungal infection. Berries with botrytis will be covered with gray fluffy mold, and the canes can also be infected, and even be killed completely in severe cases. To avoid overcrowded conditions, plant the canes at the spacing recommended for the particular variety, and prune annually. If botrytis does appear, cut off and burn the infected berries and canes as soon as you notice them. If you have had severe trouble in the past, spray with the currently approved fungicide in your home state when the first flowers open and again about two weeks later.

Crown gall: this bacterial infection attacks a wide range of plants; beets, peach, apple, plum and pear trees can be infected, as well as raspberries, loganberries and blackberries. Plants growing in wet soils or damp conditions are most vulnerable. The main symptoms are round, irregular-shaped swellings on the roots, although sometimes galls will appear on the canes. The galls can vary in size, from quite small to about 3 in (7.5 cm) or more in diameter. Sometimes the galls join together to form one enormous gall. Young galls are usually soft and white, while older ones are hard and dark in color.

Because the bacteria enter the plant through wounds either caused by hoeing or primary attack by insects, try to keep your garden pest-free, and avoid wounding with a hoe. If your soil is waterlogged, adequate correction before the blackberries are planted is another sensible precaution.

Although infected plants may continue to crop at a reduced rate, it is best to dig out and burn them, to avoid spreading the disease.

Powdery mildew: this is another fungal infection which attacks a wide variety of plants. The main symptom is a white powdery coating on the plant, usually on the stems or leaves and, sometimes, the berries.

The best preventive measure is to ensure that the plants have an adequate supply of water, and a good circulation of air. If powdery mildew does appear, cut out seriously infected canes immediately, well back to healthy growth, and spray the remainder with a fungicide approved by your own state authorities; ask your state university. Do not allow infected canes to remain on the plants.

▲ *Powdery mildew: blackberries growing in very dry soils are most vulnerable.*

Ministry of Agriculture, Fisheries and Food

GUIDE TO BLACKBERRY TROUBLES

Symptoms	Probable cause
Misshapen berries, with bright red drupelets	Redberry mite
Young shoots stunted, leaves curled	Aphids
Small, round or elongated ashy spots on canes; fruit spotted or misshapen	Anthracnose
Fruits and canes covered with fluffy gray mold	Botrytis
Round swellings on roots or canes (without tunnels)	Crown gall
White powdery coating on leaves and young cane tips	Powdery mildew
Spindling shoots, narrow young leaves, orange spores underneath	Orange rust
Double or deformed blossoms	Double blossom
Mottled foliage, weak growth not corrected by feeding	Virus diseases
Cigar-shaped galls at cane bases	Red-necked cane borer
Weak growth, hollow stems, exit holes	Raspberry crown borer
Chewed leaves	Japanese or other beetles, caterpillars, etc.

Orange rust: the symptoms are spindling shoots, narrow young growth and bright orange spores on the undersides of the leaves. A systemic disease, it travels throughout the plant, including the suckers. Dig out and burn infected plants completely, including any wild plants nearby.

Double blossom: attacks mostly evergreen sorts grown in mild climates. Deformed flowers produce no fruit. Pick off and burn infected buds, those more fleshy and reddish.

Anthracnose: produces small, ashy spots on canes, especially near their bases, sometimes encircling the canes. Spots may also appear on leaves and fruits, producing sunken gray drupelets. Apply a dormant spray. If necessary, apply an approved fungicide just before blooming and after harvest.

Virus diseases: occasionally the leaves become mottled and growth is poor. If all the plants suffer equally, it is likely to be a nutritional deficiency; apply a complete fertilizer fairly high in nitrogen and trace elements. If the symptoms are present the following spring, it is more likely to be a virus disease. Even then, destroy all your plants only if your fruit production is down seriously. If only a few plants are affected and the others are dark green and vigorous, destroy only the former and spray the remainder with an approved fungicide as a possible precaution.

Red-necked cane borer: if cigar-shaped swellings appear near the bases of the canes, prune out these galls and burn during the regular dormant pruning.

Raspberry crown borer: if growth is weak and the old canes are seen to be hollow, perhaps with exit holes when pruned out, spray the bases of the canes with Sevin or malathion in October and again a few weeks later, look for clearwing moths and mustard seed eggs at the margins and undersides of the leaves— boring starts at the top.

Japanese and other beetles, caterpillars, etc.: if broad, iridescent beetles appear, or other beetles or caterpillars, and chew the leaves, spray as needed with Sevin or malathion.

growing ideas

Different and Delicious Berries

Sweet, juicy blueberries grow well where other fruit may not flourish and they provide a delicious change for your jams, pies and cakes.

Blueberries are a tasty and ornamental fruit which deserve to be more widely grown than they are at present. They thrive on rather acid ground, where some berries may not do well, so they are an excellent choice if your garden is on light, acid, sandy soil. Blueberries grow in clusters on bushy shrubs, which have a brilliant autumn leaf color. The small, white, bell-shaped flowers, which smell as sweet as cowslips, appear in mid-spring. They open in succession over a period of several weeks, which helps to diminish damage from frost.

The blueberry most suitable to the home fruit grower is the North American high-bush type (*Vaccinium corymbosum*), which grows to about 6 ft (1.8 m) or more tall, and a few specialist fruit nurseries now offer bushes. However, there are a number of other, harder-to-come-by, edible species of the *Vaccinium* genus, as well as a number with sour fruits such as the cowberry and the cranberry. The low-bush blueberry (*V. augustifolium*) produces small, very sweet fruits, and it will tolerate quite cold climates. Its height is about 1 ft (30 cm). By contrast, the rabbiteye blueberry (*V. ashei*) grows freely in southern areas where the summers are warm and the winters are short.

When choosing a site for your blueberries, consider first if you have had success growing rhododendrons, or if they thrive in your area. Blueberries need similar conditions, and they should grow well where rhododenrons grow. The ideal site is on flat or gently sloping land with an open aspect and free air circulation, although somewhat sheltered from strong winds.

You should never grow blueberries with other fruit, and do not use the same fruit cage. Blueberries will not tolerate the lime which many other fruits must have.

If your soil is not acid, do not attempt blueberries, as you will never get a good crop. A soil test should give a pH of 4 to 5.5. The best soil is light sand or one high in peat content, moisture-retentive but well drained.

If you are incorporating a tract of wild land into your garden for the first time, it is a good idea to use a tiller to do the heaviest work. This will also help to turn in and bury heavy growths which will then create an ideal rooting medium. The warm, dry summer months are the best time to do this preparation. Clear the site thoroughly and completely of weeds, especially perennial ones, as the bushes will be down for at least 30 years.

Plant blueberries any time in autumn in mild areas, and in early spring in cold areas, spaced 6 x 6 ft (1.8 x 1.8 m). Although a single bush will form fruit, your crops will be increased if you plant two or more varieties together; you can expect up to 5–10 lb (2.5–4.5 kg) fruit per bush, picked over a period of several weeks. Buy healthy two-year-old bushes, which will be about 1 ft (30 cm) high.

Michael Warren

▲ *A well-grown high-bush variety with a full crop of blueberries ready for picking.*

Prepare the soil at least a month in advance of planting. If your soil lacks organic matter, spread sphagnum peat 3 in (7.5 cm) deep over the area to be planted, and mix it in while digging. At the same time, dress the soil with rotted garden compost or manure at about 12 lb per sq yd (5½ kg per sq m).

To plant, dig a hole big enough to contain the natural spread of the roots, and place the plant in it to the same depth as its nursery planting. Crumble the soil back over the roots until the hole is filled, and then mulch around the bush with sawdust 4 or 5 in (10 or 13 cm) thick. A 1 oz (30 g) application of a complete fertilizer sprinkled around each bush before mulching will be useful. Staking is not required. No pruning after planting is needed, but if the plants attempt to flower the first spring, the flowers should be removed. Blueberries make a slow start, but once established they are long-lived, fruiting for at least 30 years.

Care and cultivation for blueberries is similar to other bush fruits, although they require far less care than many other fruits. If the soil around the plants is heavily mulched every spring with peat or sawdust, watering will be necessary only in hot, dry summers, and weeding will be minimal. If weeds do appear, they are likely to be perennial, so destroy them immediately and completely. Keep a watch for and remove any blackberry seedlings which may appear; birds are the culprits and frequently drop them near the bushes.

Feeding the plants and mulching the soil is important in caring for blueberries. In spring, mulch with a 4 in (10 cm) deep layer of sawdust or peat to help retain moisture and stimulate growth.

Different and Delicious Berries   *135*

mulching with sawdust

Extra nitrogen will be needed if you have used sawdust. Spread over the sawdust 1½ oz (45 g) sulfate of ammonia or 2 oz (60 g) of dried blood, but use half these quantities where peat is the mulch. Add 1 oz (30 g) of sulfate of potash at the same time. In midsummer, a further application of the nitrogenous manures may be needed if the soil is particularly poor.

Growth of blueberries takes place in two stages, and it is important to recognize these. First, sideshoots grow from below the flower clusters which formed the previous year. These cease to grow temporarily in early summer, and then resume growth to form flower buds. The second stage of growth begins in midsummer, when new shoots thrust from the woody crown at ground level; by late autumn these may be 6 ft (1.8 m) high, with the top 10 in (25 cm) covered with potential fruiting buds. Fruit is carried only on the previous year's shoots, either the new, long growths from the ground, or the sideshoots from the growth completed the year before. Blueberries require some pruning, but it should not begin in earnest until the third year after planting, when the original branches of the young bush have become dry and twiggy.

Each winter or early spring, starting with the third one, cut out the oldest stems which have borne two crops, that is, all the stems which have branches that have completed fruiting. Cut them back to the base, or to a strong, low side-shoot if there is one. This will encourage strong new growth and heavy cropping. Also remove straggling shoots close to the ground and if there are many new shoots from the base, thin them out a little to get some space and air into the bush. Prune moderately and by about the same amount each year if possible. The removal of too much growth can shock the bush into producing a lot of strong new shoots at the expense of fruit and vice versa. If the summer was dull and cold, it may also be necessary to prune back any green soft growth from the tip. Cut until you reach hard brown wood.

You will be able to harvest your first small crop of blueberries the second summer after planting, although the maximum cropping potential of 10 lb (4.5 kg) per bush will not be reached for another two to six years. Pick the clusters, starting in midsummer, when they are firm and very dark blue. You should manage four or five pickings in a season, extending into early autumn. Roll the berries off with your thumb and forefinger, dropping the stalks at the same time.

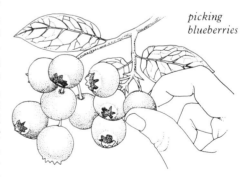

picking blueberries

When picking has finished, clear out any weeds and debris on the ground, and renew the mulch if necessary.

Blueberries make a delicious dessert eaten fresh with sugar and cream, or you can use them in cakes, pies, biscuits or tarts. Blueberry jam is superb, and they are an excellent fruit for canning or freezing.

Broccoli

Brassica oleracea botrytis cymosa (fam. *Cruciferae*)
Hardy or half-hardy perennial, grown as an annual, biennial or perennial
Sowing to harvesting time: 11–14 weeks
Size: varies greatly, but may reach 3 ft (90 cm); maximum diameter of plants with mature heads 18 in (45 cm)
Yield: up to 2 lb (.9 kg) per plant

Broccoli is one of the most delicious and easy-to-grow members of the cabbage family. By planting twice you can have early summer and fall crops. The edible portion of sprouting broccoli is similar to cauliflower but, instead of forming one large head, most varieties produce a mass of smaller ones on many side shoots. Each of these small heads consists of a curd (tight mass of flower buds) at the end of a soft stalk.

There are three main types of sprouting broccoli: purple, white (rarely grown in the United States), and green or Calabrese. All three types originated in southern Europe, purple and white coming from the north of Italy and Calabrese from the region of Calabria in southern Italy. Calabrese is slightly less hardy than the purple and white varieties.

Sprouting broccoli is cultivated in much the same way as other brassicas, such as cabbages, cauliflower and Brussels sprouts, and the rules of crop rotation observed for brassicas apply to sprouting broccoli as well.

Suitable site and soil
Although it is fairly tough, broccoli appreciates a sunny sheltered position and will grow better in these conditions. Avoid sites that are low-lying or subject to flooding in winter. As with other brassicas, a fairly heavy soil is best, although pure clay is obviously not suitable. Broccoli tolerates a wide range of soil types however, provided drainage is good, and will grow on light sandy soil if it has been properly enriched. The soil must be fertile to get good crops; soil which has been well manured for a previous crop is suitable. If the soil is poor or has not been recently manured, it is worthwhile digging in manure to be more sure of a good harvest.

Work in manure, at the rate of one large bucket per sq yd (sq m), in late autumn or early winter, prior to planting. This gives the soil time to settle and become firm before the broccoli is put in. Unless the soil is already limey, work in ground lime at the rate indicated by taking a soil test. Two full weeks before planting apply a general fertilizer at the

PREPARATION AND SOWING

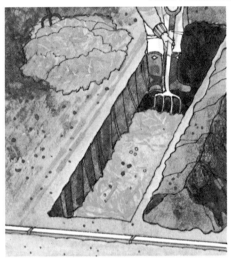

1. In late autumn or early spring, work in well-rotted manure at the rate of one bucket per sq yd (sq m).

2. Two weeks before sowing, apply a complete fertilizer at the rate of 3 oz per sq yd (90 g per sq m).

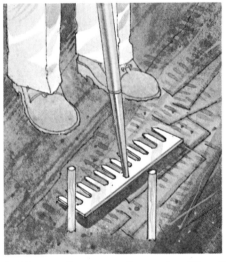

3. For direct sowing in seed beds, make shallow drills 6 in (15 cm) apart and ½ in (1.3 cm) deep; sow thinly.

4. After sowing, cover the seeds with soil and firm down the bed with the back of a rake.

rate of 3 oz per sq yd (90 g per sq m), and fork it in lightly.

Sowing

The early crop is best started indoors 4–5 weeks before setting out and is then placed in a spot outdoors where the soil becomes workable early in the season. Late crops are direct-seeded outdoors in late spring or early summer for fall or early winter harvest. Where winters are sufficiently mild they can be left for later, even spring harvesting. A packet frequently contains enough seed for

THINNING AND TRANSPLANTING

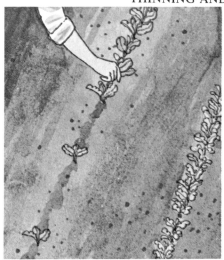

1. For plants sown directly in their final position, thin to a spacing of 2½-3 ft (75-90 cm).

2. To transplant indoor-started broccoli, lift plants from flat, retaining as much soil as possible around roots.

3. Transplanting is best done in wet weather; dig holes 2-2½ ft (60-75 cm) apart and carefully insert plants.

4. Dust transplanted sprouting broccoli with approved control as protection against club root.

100–300 plants, so use it sparingly. Sow the seeds thinly, about ½ in (1.3 cm) deep. If the seedlings are too crowded, they will be distorted, with slender, elongated growth. For seed sown where the plants are to grow, leave 3 ft (90 cm) between the rows. Temperature required for germination is from 40–84° F (4–29° C), and the period of germination, from the date of sowing, is from seven to twelve days. When the seedlings have appeared, dress them with flea beetle dust such as pyrethrum, rotenone or Sevin, and thin out the young plants to

Step-by-step Growing Guide for Broccoli

CULTIVATION

1. Keep the plants well watered in dry weather; use a fine rose on your watering can.

2. Mulch with garden compost to aid weed control, to prevent the soil from drying out and to feed the plants.

3. When top dressing, sprinkle the fertilizer evenly around the plant in a circle the size of top growth.

4. In autumn, earth-up the varieties that have to withstand winter to a height of 4 in (10 cm) around the stem.

3 in (7.5 cm) apart when they are large enough to handle.

If you have sown seeds in a seed bed, and are transplanting the young plants to their final positions, lift them when they have four to five true leaves. Transplant them carefully and firmly, during showery weather if possible. Make sure you retain a reasonable size ball of soil around the roots. If the soil is dry, dig a hole for each plant and flood it with water prior to transplanting.

For direct-sown seedlings, thin them so that there is 2 ft, 6 in–3 ft (75–90 cm)

HARVESTING

1. When harvesting, cut the main head first, to encourage the growth of smaller green heads.

2. The side shoots are removed next, to stimulate further growth. Always pick while flower buds are closed.

3. Harvest flowering shoots from the top downward; snap off the first 6 in (15 cm) of each.

between plants, as soon as they are large enough to handle.

Cultivation
If broccoli has been firmly planted in well-prepared soil, cultivation requirements are modest. They must be kept well watered in dry weather and free of weeds. A mulch of garden compost or farmyard manure will aid in weed control and will also help prevent the soil from drying out. Do not over-fertilize the soil, however, as that encourages soft and sappy growth which can be damaged by cold weather. For this reason, avoid using unnecessary applications of nitrate of soda or sulfate of ammonia.

Check the plants regularly for caterpillars; remove and destroy any you find. Top dress at monthly intervals with a good complete fertilizer at the rate of 1 oz per sq yd (30 g per sq m); this improves the quality of the flower heads for eating.

In autumn, earth-up round the stems of varieties which are to hibernate in the open. Gently pack soil around the base of the plants to a height of 4 in (10 cm) above ground level. This gives the plants better anchorage to withstand strong winds, and also gives some protection from frost.

Harvesting
For the best eating quality, pick the curds of all varieties of broccoli before

Step-by-step Growing Guide for Broccoli   *141*

AFTERCARE AND STORING

1. After harvesting a crop of heads from repeating sorts, mulch with garden compost or farmyard manure.

2. After cropping, dig up and burn the tough woody stems; this helps prevent the spread of disease.

the flower buds have opened. The curds develop and flower very quickly, particularly if the weather is good, so inspect the plants daily as they begin to reach maturity.

Cut off and eat the central curds first; this encourages the plant to produce smaller green heads in succession. Pick these curds with 6 in (15 cm) of stem.

Christmas Purple Sprouting broccoli is a late variety, and is usually harvested in early winter. Harvest the central shoots first and the plant will continue to send up smaller side shoots, which form the second, third and fourth pickings. Snap off the shoots when they are 5–6 in (12.5–15 cm) long; leave 2 in (5 cm) of stalk to develop another crop of shoots. Do not pick off the leaves at the base of the stalk; they help to protect the new shoots. When the last crop of shoots has been picked, these basal leaves can be harvested and used as greens.

If you have an unexpected glut of sprouting broccoli, and more curds are ready for picking than you can use, pick only as much as you need for immediate use.

If you wish to keep broccoli for two to

3. To store broccoli for up to 3 weeks, dig up the plant and hang upside down in a cool place.

three weeks after it is harvested, pull up the plants, including the roots. Hang them upside down in a cool place, perhaps a cellar or shed. Most are excellent for freezing.

When you have finished cropping, dig up and burn all stalks. This practice

Jerry Tubby

▲ *Broccoli plants and others of cabbage family under netting for protection against birds.*

helps prevent the spread of pests and diseases.

Exhibition tips

Because most varieties of sprouting broccoli are ready for picking from early autumn through midspring, they are not usually seen in summer exhibitions. However if you do exhibit them, eighteen heads is the number frequently displayed. Pick the shoots the evening before the show, and wrap them in damp cloths or sacking. To avoid wilting, store them in a cool dark place. Before the show, cut all the shoots to the same length. Generally, select young, healthy and unblemished curds; trim, wash and arrange them in as attractive a manner as possible.

Freezing tips

Broccoli, like all vegetables, is best frozen as soon as possible after it is picked. Select tight, compact, dark-green heads with tender stalks that are free from woodiness. Trim off large leaves and tough parts of stems; wash thoroughly. If necessary, soak stalks for half an hour in salt water to remove insects.

Cut broccoli lengthwise into uniform pieces leaving heads about 1½ in (3.8 cm) across. Steam for five minutes or boil for three minutes, then cool by plunging into cold water. When cool, pack so some heads are at each end of the container—to get more broccoli in each package. No head space is needed. Be sure to label with contents and date. Freeze at once.

R. J. Corbin

➧ *Christmas Purple Sprouting, many small heads. White Sprouting, popular abroad.* ➤

Varieties

Bravo: produces immense central heads on compact plants; a favorite commercial sort in Canada, northern United States.

Cleopatra: good flavor, uniform maturity; vigorous laterals. Stands cold, drought.

Christmas Purple Sprouting: late and hardy; extends season. Many small heads.

DeCicco: early, deep green; large central head, many side shoots. Good in South, too.

Green Hornet: 5 days earlier than Premium Crop. Central head early, few side shoots—for one-shot harvesting, good for freezing.

Pat Brindley

Early Bird: hybrid, very early, resists mildew; good market type.

Green Comet Hybrid: ripens with Green Hornet; dwarf, medium head with laterals.

➤*Green Comet has one medium head.*

▼*Rapine, or Spring Raab (left), is ideal for spring planting. England's Nine Star Perennial (right).*

Thompson & Morgan Ltd.

Brian Furner

Brian Furner

Green Duke Hybrid: early; heads medium large, tight. Good flavor.

Green Mountain: main to late crop, blue-green; resists bolting. Stands short seasons, cold nights.

Italian Sprouting (Calabria): main crop, heavy yielder, large head, medium laterals.

Raab Salad: best planted in fall; needs cold to crop. Slow.

Brian Furner

⬆ *Leaves of this plant have been attacked by pigeons; netting is the best protection.*

Pests & Diseases

Sometimes it is necessary to resort to chemicals to rid a garden of pests and diseases. However, you can try to prevent them from getting a foothold. Remove diseased plants immediately so the disease does not spread—and don't handle healthy plants until you have washed your hands thoroughly. Broccoli is affected by the same diseases as other members of the cabbage family. As many of the pests and disease organisms build up in the soil in a cumulative manner, it is important to practice crop rotation. Ideally, brassicas must not be grown on the same soil more than once in three years.

Premium Crop Hybrid: dwarf, main crop; heads large, few side shoots. Single harvest for freezing, canning.

Rapine (Spring Raab): quick, for early spring planting; branching, no central head. Bolts; likes steady moisture.

Regal F-1: a second-early; heads large unless crowded, few leaves. Resists disease, especially mildew.

Spartan Early: low, uniform; large head. Popular in North.

Special Early One: Large head, few laterals; for spring in Northeast especially.

Waltham 29: dwarf, slow, for late fall harvest. Large heads, numerous laterals; good for freezing.

Other varieties
Nine Star Perennial: popular in England, produces six or seven creamy-white heads per year for several years.

Express Corona: very early cropping variety that is ready from late summer onward abroad; heavy cropper.

Late White Sprouting: is prolific cropper abroad, snow white heads like mini-cauliflower produced from midspring.

Cabbage maggot: the maggots of gray root flies are active from late spring until late summer, with usually more than one generation. The maggots emerge from eggs laid by female flies and then burrow in to the roots. They chew off the side roots of brassicas, leaving only the tap roots. Infested plants will have wilted, faded leaves, particularly in dry weather. The plants will either die, or become stunted and yield poor crops.

Because the female flies are attracted to the smell of freshly planted brassicas, it is a good idea to mulch the area with fresh compost. The smell of the compost is stronger than the smell of brassicas, and the flies will be less likely to lay eggs there. Also, place tarpaper collars flat on ground around stems.

Flea beetle: these usually dark pests eat small circular holes in the leaves of young plants; seedlings are particularly vulnerable. Flea beetles are most active in fine weather during mid and late spring. Because the beetles hibernate in rubbish, woodpiles, or similar places, keep your garden free of such as a preventative measure. Flea beetles feed on weeds of the *Cruciferae* family, such as shepherd's purse, so also keep your garden weed-free. Pyrethrum, rotenone or Sevin used as a dust or spray will give some protection to young seedlings.

▲ The symptoms of club root disease: swollen roots with gall-like growths.

▲ Ring spot is a fungal disease. Weak plants are most vulnerable.

Cabbage caterpillars: these pests are the larval stage of the cabbage butterfly and the cabbage moth. The cabbage butterfly lays its yellow eggs in clusters on the leaves; the emerging green caterpillars feed on the heads and leaves until they are skeletonized. The caterpillars also foul the remaining leaves with excrement. The caterpillars of the cabbage moth are light green at first, changing to dark green, brown, or black as they mature. These are more difficult to control than the cabbage butterfly caterpillars, as they burrow into the heads of sprout-

ing broccoli, and are not usually discovered until it is too late.

Green-curded varieties of sprouting broccoli are particularly vulnerable to attack, because it is difficult to see the green caterpillars in and on the green flower bud.

Look for the eggs on the leaves and destroy them by crushing them between your fingers; eggs are usually laid on the undersides of leaves. Remove and destroy any caterpillars you find. If there are too many caterpillars to be controlled by hand picking, spray with pyrethrum, rotenone or Sevin according to manufacturer's instructions.

Birds: pigeons are usually the most troublesome birds, particularly in winter; they strip the leaf tissue from the plants. Netting the plants is the best solution, although a scarecrow may give temporary protection.

Cabbage aphid: these insects are also called mealy aphid; they are grayish-white and waxy in appearance. They feed on the sap and leaves, which then become curled, discolored and blistered. In bad attacks young plants can be killed. The aphids also produce honeydew, which encourages sooty mold.

Some years are much worse than others for cabbage aphids; they are most likely to be troublesome during warm dry summers. Because cabbage aphids lay eggs on old cabbage and Brussels sprouts stalks, make sure you dig these up immediately after harvesting and burn them. Do not put them on the compost heap. Inspect the plants; remove and burn infested leaves before the attack builds up. In severe cases of infestation, spray with malathion or Sevin.

Club root: this is the most serious disease likely to affect broccoli. It is caused by a soil fungus; the above-ground symptoms are wilting in hot weather and severe stunting. The roots, when dug up, will be swollen, with large gall-like growths. The inside of the gall is mottled or discolored, or has an unpleasant odor. Burn all infected plants; do not leave them in the ground or put them on the compost heap.

The only way to get rid of the fungus which causes club root is to starve it out. Make sure you rotate your crops, and do not plant the cabbage family in the garden for three years if club root is present. Get rid of all weeds of the *Cruciferae* family, such as shepherd's purse, as they harbor the disease.

Because acid, badly drained soil encourages club root, correct drainage and acidity before planting. Do not apply acidic fertilizers. Once the soil is infected, liming will help get rid of the disease, but it is a slow process, and may take up to 18 months to be fully effective. Apply ground lime at the necessary rate to bring the pH up to neutral.

Downy mildew: the symptoms of this fungal disease are white patches, usually on the undersides of the leaves. As with club root and cabbage aphid, shepherd's purse is a host plant, so make sure your garden is weed free. If badly infected, spray the plants with a recommended fungicide.

Blackleg: a fungus similar to damping off in seedlings which can infect young plants. Infected seedlings collapse at ground level and die. Young plants develop hard brown stem bases. It is most

▲ Caterpillars can be very damaging; they eat leaves until they are skeletonized.

likely to occur in wet, overcrowded conditions; to prevent, thin seedlings before they become overcrowded and avoid overwatering. Treating the soil with a recommended control prior to sowing helps.

Ring spot: this fungal disease appears as round, pale brown spots on the lower leaves. The leaves then turn yellow and drop off. Heavily manured plants and those which have weak lush growth are most vulnerable. The best precaution is to grow sprouting broccoli as part of a crop rotation plan and harden the growth with a potash dressing.

GUIDE TO BROCCOLI TROUBLES

Symptoms	Probable causes
Wilted, purple leaves	Cabbage maggot
Small circular holes in leaves	Flea beetle
Leaves skeletonized, curds eaten, fouled with excrement	Cabbage caterpillars
Leaf tissues stripped from plants	Birds
Leaves curled, discolored and blistered	Cabbage aphid
Plants wilted, stunted, roots swollen and rotten	Club root
White patches on undersides of leaves	Downy mildew
Seedlings collapse, older plants have brown, hard stem bases	Blackleg
Small, brown spots on lower leaves	Ring spot

Brussels Sprouts

Brassica oleracea gemmifera (fam. *Cruciferae*)
Hardy biennial, usually grown as an **annual**
Sowing to harvesting time: 14–17 weeks
Size: about 3 ft (90 cm) tall
Yield: 6 plants per 10 ft (3 m) row, each producing about 1 lb (½ kg) of sprouts

Brussels sprouts—firm, tight, buttonlike miniature cabbages—are one of the most highly prized of all winter vegetables. These brassicas were practically created for growing in the cool, temperate climates where many other vegetables do not thrive, and they are fairly straightforward to grow. The recent introduction of F₁ hybrids has all but eliminated the once common problem of "blown" sprouts, those with open and leafy rather than tight heads. The flavor of these new varieties is also an improvement, making Brussels sprouts an even more important choice for your garden.

A descendant of the wild cabbage and closely related to Savoy cabbage, Brussels sprouts have a growth habit quite different from other brassicas. The stem of the plant is crowned by a head of inward-curling leaves. From the crown almost down to the base of the stem are closely packed leaf joints, and careful plant breeding has ensured that tight little cabbagelike heads are produced in these joints all the way up the stem. Each of these miniature cabbages is called a sprout. Tradition says that the vegetable originated in the area of northern Europe which is now Belgium, and takes its name from the capital city. It is an economical vegetable to grow, as both the leafy tops and the sprouts make delicious vegetables.

With most brassicas, the buds in the leaf joints do not form until the second season of growth, but Brussels sprouts develop theirs during the first year. The natural tendency of the plant is to form sprouts near the base and then in turn up the stem. After those formed first at the bottom have been picked, the sprouts further up the stem grow bigger, so that a succession of pickings can be made from the same plant. For quite a long time, plants were developed which would produce greater quantities of large sprouts. However, large sprouts have less flavor, and the trend now, started by the commercial growers, is to grow plants which produce a mass of small to medium-sized sprouts, all of which come to maturity at about the same time.

It is a good idea to decide what you

Picturepoint

▲ *Brussels sprouts—firm, miniature cabbages—are a popular winter vegetable.*

plan to do with your sprouts before choosing your varieties. For general kitchen use, you will probably want a variety which grows fairly large and produces a succession of sprouts throughout the winter. However, if you plan to freeze most of your crop, choose a commercial growers' variety so that all the sprouts will be ready for harvest and preparation at once. Remember, too, that the picking season can be extended by using a range of varieties which will come into production at different times. The harvesting season for sprouts is from early autumn through to early spring. There are some extra early varieties which will begin to crop in late summer, but, unless you are extremely fond of sprouts, it is rather a waste to begin harvesting them at a time when so many other seasonal vegetables are at their peak.

Brussels sprouts are one of the best cool-climate crops. They are hardy and will withstand considerable frost, although they will not tolerate extreme heat. A hot, dry summer seems to inhibit their capacity to produce tight sprouts in the following autumn. In the initial stages the seeds and young plants need a temperature well above the freezing point, but in the following winter the mature plants will stand quite severe and prolonged frost. The plants will not grow during such extreme conditions, but they will remain alive and will resume growth when the frost is past.

Suitable site and soil
Brussels sprouts are not particular about soil requirements. They will grow in almost any type of soil, although they do best in a good deep loam. If the soil is at all acid, correct with an application of lime during the winter, otherwise you may run into trouble with a disease such as club root.

When choosing your site, remember that sprouts can grow into tall plants, and that they will occupy their position for quite a long time. If possible, try to arrange the rows so that the sprouts do not block the sunlight from other crops. A site in full sunlight is not essential, as long as it gets sun for part of the day. And since Brussels sprouts are top-heavy plants, avoid a site which will get the full force of the wind, or be sure to give some wind protection.

Since Brussels sprouts are brassicas, do not plant them in a site previously occupied by another brassica crop, or pests and diseases may build up in the soil. A site last occupied by peas or beans is a good choice. In fact, any position, not recently planted to a member of the cabbage family, which was manured for a previous crop is good. But if this is not possible, dig the site deeply and work in

a heavy dressing of well-rotted farmyard manure or garden compost as early as possible in the autumn before planting. This will allow time for the soil to settle and become firm, which is very important if you wish to avoid blown sprouts. If you did not manure the site in the previous autumn, apply a top-dressing of a complete fertilizer (which has slightly more potash and phosphate than nitrogen in it) at the rate of 3–4 oz per sq yd (90–120 g per sq m), about seven to ten days before planting.

Sowing the seed
Brussels sprouts can be sown in a seedbox, in boxes under glass or outdoors in a seedbed and then transplanted to their final positions. Transplanting seems to strengthen the plants and gives an improved crop.

Any available plot of fairly fine soil will do for a seedbed, as the plants will only be there for a few weeks. Rake the soil over lightly, and make drills about ½ in (1.3 cm) deep, and 6–9 in (15–22.5 cm) apart. For a maincrop of sprouts, sow the seed in midspring. Like all brassica seed, that of Brussels sprouts is small and round; sow seeds quite thinly. Germination should take place within seven to twelve days of sowing, a little longer if the weather is cold. If you have any seed left over, keep it, as it should remain viable for three years.

For sowing in containers, choose standard-sized seed flats or pots filled with a good quality seed mixture. Sow as you would for seeds in the open ground, and keep the containers indoors or in an unheated greenhouse.

You can also make sowings in frames or under protective covers. Again, follow the instructions for sowing in the open ground. For frame cultivation, water the soil thoroughly before sowing if it is not already moist, so that further watering is unnecessary during the seedling stage. If sown under frames or covers, the plants can be thinned and then left in their original positions to mature if you do not wish to transplant them, but remember that the plants may not be as good in the

Step-by-step Growing Guide for Brussels Sprouts

STARTING UNDER GLASS

1. **In mid to late winter, sow seeds directly in a cold frame; cover with a thin layer of finely sifted soil.**

2. **In the greenhouse, sow seeds ½ in (1.3 cm) deep in a seed flat filled with good quality seed mixture.**

3. **As soon as the seedlings show the first pair of leaves, prick them out from seed boxes into pots or flats.**

4. **Harden young plants off; place pots in a cold frame outdoors and open top on mild, sunny days.**

long run. If the seed is sown outdoors without any protection with glass or plastic, cover with netting at once; birds, especially pigeons and sparrows, are very fond of the plants both when young and mature.

Planting out

As a general rule, young Brussels sprout plants should remain in the seedbed, without pricking out, until ready for transplanting. They will need thinning, probably twice, so that they are spaced about 4 in (10 cm) apart before moving.

Some gardeners transplant most of the crop, but leave a few plants where they were sown, spaced about 1½ ft (45 cm) apart. This can be satisfactory, although those plants left in their original sites will seldom be as good as those which were transplanted, as transplanting appears to benefit Brussels sprouts; the plants grow stronger and produce earlier and better crops.

The time to transplant is when the danger of hard frost is past, in spring. The plants should be between 4–6 in (10–15 cm) high, but not drawn and

PLANTING OUT

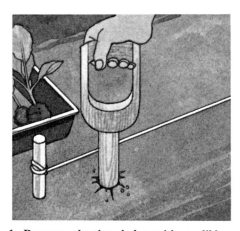

1. Prepare planting holes with a dibber when danger of hard frost is past; space plants 18 in (45 cm) apart.

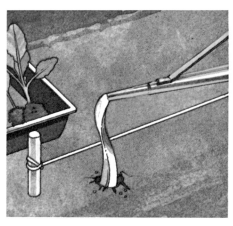

2. If the soil is dry, fill the holes with water; water the seedbed the night before transplanting.

3. Put the plants in carefully, and firm the soil around the roots with a dibber; avoid shallow planting.

4. Test for firm planting by pulling a leaf; it should just tear. If it makes the plant lift up, replant deeper.

leggy, with four or five true leaves present. It is essential to allow plenty of space between Brussels sprout plants: allow 2½–3 ft (75–90 cm) between rows with the greater spacing for the larger varieties, and 1½ ft (45 cm) between each plant in the row. It is important to plant deeply because the plants are normally shallow-rooting, and the roots have to support a tall, heavy-headed superstructure. A good rule to follow is to plant with the lower leaves just resting on the soil.

A day just after or just before a heavy rain is the best time to transplant. If this is not possible, or in a particularly dry season, water the site thoroughly first. If you can water the seedbed the night before, so much the better, as the plants will then be well watered. Prepare planting holes with a dibber and fill these with water as well. Put the plants in carefully to the correct depth, and firm the ground well around them to anchor the roots and encurge the development of tight button sprouts. Protect the plants from bird attacks; it is a good idea to have them netted or in a permanent cage.

Step-by-step Growing Guide for Brussels Sprouts

▲ *Birds can do a great deal of damage; protect plants with netting if needed.*

A-Z Collection

Early crops

Early sprouts, ready from late summer onwards, are considered desirable by many gardeners, although this is the time of year when summer vegetables such as pole beans and cauliflowers are both plentiful and cheap.

If you are determined to have early sprouts, then sow in late winter or early spring. Because sprouts require a long period of growth, and hard frosts sometimes occur in spring, you will have to sow the seeds under glass. For germination to take place, the temperature of the soil must be 50–55° F (10–13° C). When the winter is mild you can use an unheated greenhouse or conservatory indoors, or sow them outdoors under frames. If the winter is particularly cold, either delay sowing until the weather warms up and accept that early crops will not be possible, or use a heated greenhouse.

Sow the seed in boxes filled with a good quality seed mixture. As soon as the seedlings show the first pair of leaves, they are pricked out, or transferred from seed boxes to pots or flats which, like the seed boxes, also need the protection of glass or plastic. The seed boxes, pots or flats should contain a fine soil or potting mixture. Transplant the seedlings 2 in (5 cm) apart in all directions.

If you use flats or pots, you can place them outside the greenhouse, or open the frame cover on mild days to allow the plants to harden off. Plant them into their final positions in early to mid-spring, depending on your climate and their degree of maturity. They may continue to need protection at night if the weather is very cold.

To sow the seed directly in a cold frame, prepare the soil by watering it thoroughly so that further watering will not be necessary for some time. Sow the seed thinly in mid- to late winter and cover with ⅛ in (0.3 cm) of fine soil. Close the top or sash and cover it with a mat until germination has taken place;

CULTIVATION AND CARE

1. **Water young plants in dry weather; insufficient watering will result in blowsy, loose, unattractive buttons.**

2. **In autumn, earth up around the plants to level of lowest leaves, to protect against wind-rock and frost.**

on warm sunny days, open the frame so that air can circulate around the plants. They will still need protection in periods of heavy rain or extreme cold, particularly if frost threatens at night, when the mat should be replaced also. Thin them to about 4 in (10 cm) apart in all directions, and plant them out when plants and season are ready. Remember your bird protection.

In areas which have a mild winter, the seed is sown in sheltered borders in late summer or autumn and the plants set out in the fall or early spring. The main drawback with autumn planting is that autumn-sown plants are somewhat more likely to bolt (run to seed) without producing sprouts. Also, an unexpectedly cold winter can bring disaster to the crop.

Care and development
Remember that sprouts need plenty of water when young, and blowsy, loose buttons often result due to insufficient water at this stage. In hot, dry weather this is particularly important.

A mulch of rotted garden compost or farmyard manure put around the plants about a month after planting will help to keep the soil moist and supply a little more plant food. If you give too much

nitrogen while the plants are growing, it may result in blown sprouts later, so any addition of complete fertilizers should be done with caution, and in general only if the soil is very light and quick draining. Avoid sulfate of ammonia and nitrate of soda completely, as they are very rich in nitrates—excessive applications could quickly ruin both taste and quality of your sprouts.

Summer care consists mainly of keeping the surrounding soil free from weeds. Remember, though, that the roots of Brussels sprouts are very shallow and also widespread, so hand weeding is best. If you do hoe, hoe lightly and shallowly across the surface to avoid damage. If any leaves at the bottom of the plant become yellowed or decayed, remove them immediately or infection may spread to the sprouts and damage the crops.

If the sprouts are a tall-growing variety, or if they are on a windy site, stake the plants in early autumn, placing the stake on the windward side. Two ties are usually necessary. It also helps if you earth-up around the plants to the level of the lowest leaves at this time. Earthing-up, besides protecting the plants from wind-rock, throws excess moisture away from the stems.

Harvesting

You can encourage the formation and early maturity of sprouts by removing the top 1 in (2.5 cm) of growing tip. Do this in late summer or early autumn for maincrop varieties and late autumn for late croppers. This practice, however, tends to decrease the yield. As the crop reaches maturity the lower leaves of the plant will start to yellow. Cut or pull them off—they should come off easily if pulled downward.

Sprouts mature from the bottom of the stem upwards, and should be picked in that order. If you leave sprouts on the bottom of the stem, production of new sprouts further up will be diminished, and the lower sprouts will quickly become inedible and subject to infection or infestation by pests.

Begin picking the lower sprouts when they are about 1 in (2.5 cm) in diameter, as large sprouts are not nearly as tasty as small ones. Split each sprout off the stem with a sharp, downward tug; if they do not come off easily, use a sharp knife rather than damage the stem by pulling. Spread the harvesting evenly over all the plants; never strip one plant of all sprouts, unless it is to be a once-only harvest, perhaps for freezing.

Once the sprouts towards the top of the stem are well developed, you can cut off the top leafy growth and cook it like cabbage. After the top is cut, the remaining sprouts will mature quite

HARVESTING

1. As the crop reaches maturity, the lower leaves will start to yellow; cut or pull them off when this happens.

2. Pick sprouts from the bottom of the stem upwards; split sprouts off the stem with a sharp, downward tug.

After harvesting is finished, dig up the plants. Burn the roots, to avoid risk of club root disease. Chop up the woody stems with a spade, and put them on the compost heap.

quickly. Otherwise, the top growth can be left on until all the sprouts have been harvested, and will then provide some useful "greens" in spring. Some gardeners, who want all their sprouts early and small for freezing, cut off the top several weeks before the crop is ready for picking. Most of the sprouts will then mature at the same time.

Care after harvesting
Almost every part of the Brussels sprout plant is used. The sprouts and crown are both eaten, leaving only the stout woody stem. Some gardeners leave a few stumps of Brussels sprouts in the ground over the winter, to produce early spring greens. This is generally a bad idea because the stumps provide a convenient hibernating place for brassica pests, such as whitefly and aphids. Having spent the winter on the stumps, they then come to life in spring and reinfest newly planted brassica crops.

After harvesting the sprouts and the leafy tops, the best policy is to dig the stumps completely out of the ground. Chop off and burn the root, to avoid the risk of club root. This is why it is much better to dig rather than pull up the stumps. If you pull the stumps out, the root may break off below ground level and remain in the soil to harbor pests

and diseases. The woody stem will rot in time, but should be chopped up with a spade to aid decay. It can be dug into the soil but is probably best incorporated in the compost heap.

A Brussels sprout crop is a heavy drain on soil, which will benefit from a generous manuring before being used again. Dig it in as early as possible in the autumn before planting.

Exhibition tips
Brussels sprouts when well grown can make a fine display on the show bench, whether in individual classes or part of a collection. There are no special cultivation requirements for sprouts intended for showing; good general cultivation should lead to sprouts excellent for both kitchen and show use. Fifty sprouts is a usual number required for both single dishes and collections.

Judges will look for fresh, solid and tightly closed sprouts. As with most vegetables, enormous size is not of paramount importance, and small sprouts which are tightly closed will be favored over large, loose, blowsy ones.

Try to leave the selection of the sprouts until the last possible moment. Although they will keep for several days when stored in a damp sack in a cool dark shed or cellar, they really look their

▲ *Early Morn*

▲ *Green Pearl*

best when freshly picked. To make certain that the sprouts are as uniform as possible, it is a good idea to first select one sprout as a control; it should be slightly smaller than average, no more than 1½ in (3.8 cm) in diameter and tightly closed. Using this sprout as a reference select about one hundred more. This seems like an extravagant number, but you may need a good supply of replacements at the show and it is better to have a few extra. Although they are tough, strong growers, do not handle the sprouts carelessly, or they may bruise.

Little is needed in the way of preparation. If the tiny leaves at the base of the sprouts look yellow or are otherwise unsightly, cut them off with a sharp knife. Do not pick off too many outer leaves, though, because the inner leaves are paler and less attractive. Then cut all stems to the same length, preferably short.

If the sprouts are being packed for transport to the show, make sure they are packed tightly enough; otherwise, they may bump against each other in transit and some damage may occur. If there is extra space in the box, fill it with tissue paper. The sprouts should not be left in the box too long, or the color will bleach out and rotting may occur. The usual way to display them is on a plate.

Varieties

Catskill: early, compact, uniform and productive; planted primarily as a fall crop.

Early Morn: compact, pyramidal plants of European origin; sprouts large, solid, elliptical.

Green Pearl: a European variety popular for September harvests in North. Sprouts globular, hard, uniform; plants upright, productive.

▲ *Rubine, novelty English variety.*

Indra: sprouts globular, hard; early October in North. Good for packaging.

Jade Cross: a hybrid producing twice as many sprouts as open pollinated types. Plants medium tall, upright; the most popular variety.

Long Island Improved: popular with market gardeners and home growers. Plants semidwarf; sprouts globular, medium green.

Other varieties
Rubine: novelty type abroad which produces red sprouts; very decorative plant; good flavor; ready from late autumn.

Irish Elegance: late autumn to early winter cropper abroad; good yields of medium-sized, smooth sprouts that keep well on stem for a long time.

King Arthur: popular British midseason variety; heavy crop of medium-sized, smooth skinned sprouts; plants fairly tall, uniform and hardy.

Peer Gynt: considered of outstanding quality abroad; dwarf growing and ideal for small gardens; very prolific cropper of uniform, high quality, dark green sprouts; early crops from autumn.

▲ Long Island Improved

▲ Jade Cross

Pests & Diseases

Cabbage aphids: these insects are most troublesome following mild winters. The gray aphids infest the undersides of the leaves of sprouts, which then become curled, blistered and discolored. Because the eggs of cabbage aphids spend the winter on the stumps of old brassicas, the best preventive measure is to dig up and either burn or compost the stems immediately after harvesting. Keep the plants well supplied with water, and for severe attacks, remove the worst affected leaves and sprouts and spray the remainder with rotenone or pyrethrum.

Cabbage root fly: these flies are most active from midspring through to early summer. The eggs are deposited on or just below the soil surface next to the stems, and the emerging white legless maggots burrow into the stem, and also eat the roots underground. The first obvious symptoms of cabbage root fly infestation are gray-green, wilted leaves and slow-growing plants, smaller than the others. If pulled out of the ground, the roots will be found to contain the maggots, or they may be in the soil around the roots. Surrounding the stems with a small square of roofing paper on the soil when planting will prevent egg

▲ *Cabbage aphid damage: infested leaves become curled, blistered, and discolored.*

▲ *Brussels sprout plant infected with club root, a soil-borne fungal disease.*

laying. If an infestation occurs, remove and burn damaged plants, as well as the soil around the roots.

Cabbage whitefly: these tiny white moth-like insects feed on the undersides of leaves. They are usually a problem in warm weather. Besides weakening the plants, they exude honeydew, which encourages the growth of sooty mold; in severe cases, young plants may be destroyed. Prevent serious damage by hanging between the plants cardboard strips painted bright yellow and coated with a sticky substance to trap the insects. Drive them away with a soil mulch of aluminum foil and spray with your state-approved control as directed. Remove and burn all heavily infested leaves.

Flea beetle: if the leaves of the seedlings and young sprout plants are perforated with numerous small round holes, then there is probably an infestation of flea beetle. These small black insects are most active in fine weather in mid- to late spring but can also be found at intervals throughout the summer. The best preventive measure is to spray with Sevin or malathion as needed. Hoeing frequently and gently around the young plants disturbs the soil and discourages the beetles from laying eggs.

Cutworms: these grayish-brown or gray caterpillars feed at night, when they eat through the stems, severing the plant at or slightly below ground level. If your garden is weed-free and well cultivated, you are less likely to have problems with this pest; if an infestation occurs, scatter a cutworm and slug bait between the plants.

Cabbage moth/cabbage white butterfly: the green or grayish-brown caterpillars of these insects feed on the leaf tissues of all brassicas, causing widespread damage. The cabbage moth caterpillars usually attack the inner leaves, where they are not easily reached by insecticides. The caterpillars of the butterfly eat the outer leaves, and also foul the remaining foliage with excrement. Both can do a great deal of damage and ruin the plants completely. As the eggs of both pests are laid on the leaves, remove and destroy any eggs you find on the plant. They will be small and round or conical in shape, light-colored and laid in batches. If caterpillars do manage to hatch out, hand pick them off in a mild infestation; otherwise, dust or spray the infested plants with Sevin or malathion.

Club root: this is the most serious disease the home gardener is likely to encounter; it affects all members of the brassica family. It is caused by a fungus in the soil which infects the roots; the symptoms above ground are bluish and wilting leaves, and stunted, slow-growing plants. The roots, when dug up, will be swollen and distorted, black, and rotting, often with an unpleasant odor. Club root is often associated with heavy, badly-drained soils, so a good precaution is to correct any drainage problems before planting. Excessively acid soils also tend to encourage this disease, so correct the soil acidity by liming so that the pH is near neutral. Alternatively, sow the seed in sterilized soil outdoors, or in containers, or in sterilized soil in individual pots. When transplanting, dip the roots in a fungicidal solution. Because the fungus is soil-borne, if an infection occurs, the site must not be used for brassicas for at least five years—the spores have been known to survive 20 years. All infected plants must be lifted completely and burned immediately.

Blackleg: this fungal infection attacks young plants, causing the base of the stem to become constricted, turn brown and wither. If the plants are not killed outright, they remain stunted and will never fully recover. Seeds or seedbeds dusted with quintozene or thiram or watered with cheshunt compound will usually be free of attacks.

Downy mildew: the symptoms of this fungal infection are white patches on the undersides of the leaves, and yellow speckling on the upper side, followed by wilting. It is often found on seedlings and young plants under glass, or on the outside of the young buttons later in the season. Spraying with an approved mildew control should solve the problem.

Gray mold (Botrytis cinerea): this is sometimes a trouble on Brussels sprouts. Infected sprouts become soft, and eventually covered with gray furry mold. Infection occurs through a broken main leaf stalk just below the sprout, and is more likely where too much nitrogen has been supplied. Removal of the affected parts is all that need be done.

Canker: Brussels sprouts abroad may be attacked by this fungal disease which produces brown or purple spots and cankers on the stems, and results in stunting and sometimes total wilt. Destroy affected plants and do not plant again in the same site.

Ringspot: a fungal infection encountered abroad, ring spot attacks older plants and produces round, light brown spots—about ½ in (1.3 cm) in diameter—on the outer and lower leaves. Infected leaves eventually turn completely yellow and wither. Remove and destroy all infected leaves.

GUIDE TO BRUSSELS SPROUTS TROUBLES

Symptoms	Probable cause
Leaves turn gray-green and collapse; roots tunneled, with white maggots inside them	Cabbage root fly
White patches on undersides of leaves of young plants	Downy mildew
Stunted plants with narrowed brown stem bases	Blackleg
Bluish-green, wilting leaves; swollen, black rotting roots	Club root
Stem severed at or slightly below ground level	Cutworms
Small round holes in leaves of seedlings or young plants, or complete defoliation	Flea beetle
Leaves distorted, discolored; small gray insects on undersides; stickiness on leaves, sometimes black sooty patches	Cabbage aphids
Leaves skeletonized, covered with excrement	Cabbage moth/white butterfly
Soft sprouts, gray fur on outside	Gray mold